ONE HUNDRED SERMONS SHORT & Sweet

★ ★ ★

ONE HUNDRED SERMONS SHORT & Sweet

GERALD O'MAHONY

kevin mayhew

kevin mayhew

First published in Great Britain in 2014 by Kevin Mayhew Ltd
Buxhall, Stowmarket, Suffolk IP14 3BW
Tel: +44 (0) 1449 737978 Fax: +44 (0) 1449 737834
E-mail: info@kevinmayhew.com

www.kevinmayhew.com

© Copyright 2014 Gerald O'Mahony.

The right of Gerald O'Mahony to be identified as the author of this work has been asserted by him in accordance with the Copyright, Designs and Patents Act 1988.

The publishers wish to thank all those who have given their permission to reproduce copyright material in this publication.

Every effort has been made to trace the owners of copyright material and we hope that no copyright has been infringed. Pardon is sought and apology made if the contrary be the case, and a correction will be made in any reprint of this book.

All rights reserved. No part of this publication may be reproduced, stored in a retrieval system, or transmitted, in any form or by any means, electronic, mechanical, photocopying, recording, or otherwise, without the prior written permission of the publisher.

Unless stated otherwise, Scripture quotations are taken from *The New Revised Standard Version of the Bible*, copyright © 1989 Division of Christian Education of the National Council of the Churches of Christ in the USA. Used by permission. All rights reserved.

9 8 7 6 5 4 3 2 1 0

ISBN 978 1 84867 728 9
Catalogue No. 1501450

Cover design by Rob Mortonson
© Images used under licence from Shutterstock Inc.
Edited by Nicki Copeland
Typeset by Richard Weaver

Printed and bound in Great Britain

Contents

About the author		8
Introduction		9
1	Talents: a point of view	10
2	Jesus chooses his apostles	12
3	Raising the roof	14
4	Legion of demons	16
5	Bent double	18
6	Feeding the four thousand	20
7	The last word?	22
8	Birds, rock, thorns, good soil	24
9	'Come to me . . .'	26
10	Martha and Mary	28
11	Jesus' baptism and mine	30
12	Transfiguration	32
13	*'Abba!'*	34
14	Clean	36
15	The promised Shepherd	38
16	If it were possible	40
17	Jesus: the hidden years	42
18	Weeds among the wheat	44
19	Even better than being good	46
20	Nothingness blessed	48
21	How many times?	50
22	No fixed abode	52
23	'Do not judge . . .'	54
24	Alexander the coppersmith	56
25	The star comes and goes	58
26	Wine and water	60
27	The narrow gate	62
28	Change and become like children	64
29	'Feed my lambs'	66
30	Shine a light	68
31	Bread, then wine	70
32	'The truth will make you free'	72
33	The house built on rock	74

34	Who is right?	76
35	Peter the Rock	78
36	The boy cured of epilepsy	80
37	Old and new	82
38	John beheaded	84
39	Many inns	86
40	Jesus good Samaritan	88
41	Ten bridesmaids	90
42	Jesus became poor	92
43	Recognising Jesus risen	94
44	Christ died for our sins	96
45	'I am generous'	98
46	God is . . . love is	100
47	More than	102
48	You will be forgiven	104
49	'. . . your holy servant Jesus'	106
50	About Bar'abbas	108
51	Peter fears the waves	110
52	Temple curtain torn	112
53	Grateful leper	114
54	Walking on water	116
55	One day at a time	118
56	Tree always in fruit	120
57	Holy Week and Easter	122
58	From scarlet to white as snow	124
59	Two kinds of peace	126
60	Only a few saved?	128
61	Peace comes back	130
62	God is love	132
63	No taxes for the children	134
64	If they all went away . . .	136
65	Give without payment	138
66	All is well?	140
67	God shows no partiality	142
68	Firstborn	144
69	All sins forgiven	146
70	'Immediately'	148
71	Cloud of witnesses	150
72	Brother, sister and mother	152
73	Two kinds of desolation	154

74	Left hand, right hand	156
75	Own place at the table	158
76	Stone upon stone	160
77	Water and fire	162
78	The Holy Spirit will come	164
79	Calling people names	166
80	Precious	168
81	'Where you go, I will go'	170
82	Not far	172
83	When you give a banquet	174
84	Your Father feeds them	176
85	Be imitators of God	178
86	Places at table	180
87	When the Spirit of truth comes	182
88	Wings like eagles	184
89	Gift and invitation	186
90	To forgive or to retain?	188
91	Treasure hidden in a field	190
92	A sword to guard the way	192
93	Before the foundation	194
94	Wedding robe	196
95	The hairs of your head	198
96	They also serve	200
97	Mighty warrior	202
98	To the bottom of the sea	204
99	Prepared for siege	206
100	Love in return for love	208
Index of Scripture references		211
Thematic index		214

About the author

Gerald O'Mahony was born in Wigan, Lancashire, and at the age of 18 joined the Society of Jesus (the Jesuits). He was ordained priest at the age of 30 and since then has worked in two main areas: ten years as an adviser to teachers of religious education in the Archdiocese of Liverpool, and 30 years as a retreat director and writer at Loyola Hall Jesuit spirituality centre. He has always enjoyed making his sermons short and sweet, and has finally been persuaded to put some of them in print.

Introduction

A short and sweet sermon for me means a very short, encouraging word about a Bible passage that has come up in the readings of the day. These short sermons are a write-up from memory of sermons that were first given live, to a live congregation, so they are somewhat more formal than the original spoken word.

The idea of printing and publishing this collection is first of all for the reader to enjoy them and perhaps see the relevant Scripture passage in a new light. Then if it seems good, a reader who is also a minister or a preacher might wish to borrow a thought or a prayer or the whole sermon and use it with another congregation.

I have limited the Bible quotations to one or at the most two for each short sermon, although there are usually several more Scripture references in each one. Lightweight sermons are meant to be short and punchy – with usually just one main message.

Where direct quotations from the Bible are given, they have been taken from the NRSV (New Revised Standard Version) and are within the range permitted by the publishers.

ONE
Talents: a point of view

Matthew 25:14-30

The word 'talent' came into the English language from this story told by Jesus. On the face of it, the story seems to say that the more anyone uses their talents, their natural or their God-given gifts, the more they will be pleasing to God and the greater will be their reward in the afterlife. People who do not use their talents, on the other hand, or those – like the blind poet John Milton – who lose a major talent through illness, will fear to be cast into outer darkness. I would maintain that this is not the real point of the story at all.

Let me recall the outlines of the parable. A man going on a journey sends for his slaves and distributes some of his wealth for them to trade with on his behalf during his absence. To one slave he entrusts five talents, to another two talents, to yet another one talent, according as he thinks them capable of carrying out good transactions. A talent is not a coin, but a slab of gold or silver worth thousands of pounds sterling.

So the slave with five talents does well and creates another five by the time the master gets back. The master is delighted, and promises to give him much greater responsibilities for the future. Similarly, the slave with two talents manages to double the amount, and he too is promised a greater position in the household. But the one who was entrusted with just one talent brings nothing back except the one talent he was given. 'Master', he says, 'I knew that you were a harsh man, reaping where you did not sow, and gathering where you did not scatter seed; so I was afraid, and I went and hid your talent in the ground. Here you have what is yours.'

Whereupon the master calls this slave wicked and lazy, takes his one talent and gives it to the slave who already has ten talents. For this third man, it is outer darkness, and weeping and gnashing of teeth: he is a slave, remember, so the master can do what he likes with him.

One way of looking at the story is to see it as about talents. Does that mean we are called to use each and every one of the gifts God has given us to the full? Often they are mutually exclusive: for instance, a top swimmer cannot be a top tennis player, in spite of being talented at both sports; a penguin has wings and can swim but it cannot fly.

But there is another point of view, quite another way of thinking about the parable of the talents. If we decide for ourselves that God is harsh and unfeeling, along the lines of the way the third man thinks about his master, then we will spend our whole lives in fear and dread. Nothing we do will be carefree and cheerful; nothing will be enough. Daily life will already be like 'outer darkness'. I mean this life; this is to say nothing about an afterlife where we would discover too late to do anything about it how completely freeing, loving and forgiving our God is, and that we need not have been afraid.

If we decide to believe in a loving, forgiving God from today onwards, then our quality of life improves beyond measure. We can take chances, try things out, risk failure sometimes, knowing that God would prefer us to try and trust.

TWO

Jesus chooses his apostles

Mark 3:13-19

Quite early in Jesus' public life he can see that his own days are numbered. Those who disagree with his teaching will stop at nothing to silence him. So here we have Jesus, after a day's teaching by the lakeside, choosing a band of men to carry on his message when the day would come that he himself would be silenced. He calls them apostles, meaning ambassadors or messengers with a mission.

For this, so Mark tells us, Jesus leaves the lakeside, goes up the mountain nearby and calls to him those whom he wants, and they come to him. Now I know that these are like patriarchs – only 12 of them in a position of honour in the history of the Church – but I think we may still make comparisons with our own calling in our own day. We perhaps want to be an active member of our church, and we think the idea is our own, but in fact it is Jesus who wants us, and we have come to him because he has inspired in us admiration and love for himself.

And what does Jesus call the 12 to do? Mark puts it very simply: Jesus appoints the apostles 'to be with him, and to be sent out to proclaim the message' (verse 14). Does that mission apply to our own day as well? Certainly we need to know Jesus, the real Jesus, before we can be confident that we have got his message straight. We get to know him by soaking ourselves in the Gospels and the rest of the Bible – but especially the Gospels. We get to know him by living in or close to a congregation or a community that lives by his values. In these ways, in work and in prayer, we can be with him in a similar way to the way the apostles were with him.

Living with Jesus is like a base camp for an explorer. The explorer sets out on a quest but can always touch base to restore their energy and revise their plans. We are sent out by Jesus on a quest to tell people that they are reconciled: Jesus is the Son of God and we with the whole world are invited to see ourselves as Jesus' sisters and brothers, loved by God with a parent's unconditional love, and this is the gift by which to rule our lives. We are sisters and brothers of Jesus, and sisters and brothers of one another.

On this occasion Jesus also gives the apostles authority to cast out demons. Even that commission has a meaning for the average missionary or active Christian today – to you and to me. A lot of mental stress has at its root a deep insecurity, which a true understanding of the friendliness and forgivingness of God can cure. The risen Jesus promised his kind of peace to the apostles, and the apostles have passed on the same promise to us. Trusting in Jesus can bring a healing peace to make even great stresses bearable when we are yoked with him, and he with us.

THREE

Raising the roof

Mark 2:1-12

The story in today's reading comes early in Mark's Gospel. Jesus has been in the town of Capernaum before, on a Sabbath day when he taught in the synagogue and healed Simon's mother-in-law. Then, once the Sabbath was over, he healed all sorts of sick people gathered about her door. Such was the fame of Jesus in Capernaum after that Sabbath that when he comes back to the town, the house is full and there is no longer room around the door. So, as we have heard, the intrepid four carrying a paralysed man on a mat or a stretcher let the invalid down through the roof to where Jesus can see him and speak to him.

Jesus does not seem to question whether the paralytic himself has any faith, but he sees the faith of the four stretcher bearers. He then says to the paralytic, whom presumably Jesus has never in his life seen before, 'Son, your sins are forgiven.' This statement of Jesus causes shock and horror to some scribes who are present at the scene, so Jesus speaks to them and defends the words he has used. Notice that Jesus does not say, 'I have forgiven your sins,' but 'Your sins are forgiven' – namely that 'God has forgiven your sins; your sins have been forgiven by God.' Then Jesus tells the man to get up, take up his mat and go home – which he obediently does in front of them all.

Now this is a story of something Jesus did long ago to help a particular man at the request of his four friends. Is there a message still for today, for us, coming out of the same story? I think there are probably many messages of comfort in the story, but there is one in particular that I find helpful. Suppose I, or you, identify in our imagination with the man on the stretcher, lowered by his friends in front of Jesus. We are paralysed by our past failures and our past sins: we do not dare to venture much any more for fear of failing again. What does Jesus do? He says to me, 'Gerald, your sins are forgiven.' He says the same to you, using the same words but with your familiar name. He does not ask any questions; he simply states, as a matter of fact, that God has already forgiven your sins.

Then Jesus says to get up and carry on with a good life, and not to let the past paralyse you or me for the future. So often in trying to live a good life we become despondent because things do not work out as well as we wanted them to. Our unhappy feelings then drag us back into a kind of paralysis, making us unwilling to risk, unwilling to try again. To know that God has already forgiven our weakness and wants us to start again can be enough to release us from our feeling of desolation. God does not want us to succeed in our plans to please him as much as he wants us to keep on trying, confident that God will accept the will for the deed, and will love us just the same.

What God seems to want, according to this story of Jesus and the paralytic, is that we trust in God's permanent good will. More important than success is to give the world the message of God's ready and permanent forgiveness for the past and encouragement for the future.

FOUR

Legion of demons

Mark 5:1-20

I think most of us would be out of our depth if someone tortured by a thousand demons came to us for help. I think we may safely leave this poor man for Jesus to sort out, as he did so dramatically. But there are times when we can encounter people in similar difficulties, and even we ourselves can find ourselves pulled in a thousand different ways, not knowing where to turn. At such times, Jesus' method with the sick man can be applied to our own situation and be found to work.

The story seems to indicate that the man with the legion of demons inside him is suffering from what we would call manic depression, or bipolar affective disorder. The manic side of him is shown in his enormous strength – enough to break free from any kind of restraint that the authorities tried to put on him – as well as his unwillingness to wear clothes and his wild manner that makes people afraid of him. His depression is demonstrated in his preferring to live among the tombs, and his howling by day and through the night.

What does Jesus do? According to Mark's story Jesus faces up to the man and lets him shed his demons into the herd of pigs. The pigs and demons career into the water and drown, and the man gets dressed and sits quietly asking Jesus for further orders.

When I am beset by a legion of worries, what can this story of Jesus work in me to bring me to calmness and reduce my worries to no more than two? In my prayer I can imagine that I am the man with the legion – or another like him. I ask Jesus to take from me this torture of anxieties; I ask him please to drown them all in the sea, the waters of baptism which are always to hand because they never went away. My baptism reminds me that I am a personal child of God, beloved son or beloved daughter, so that my thousand anxieties are reduced to one: what one thing does God my Father, my *Abba*, want me to do next?

Not many people suffer from bipolar disorder, but nearly everybody experiences changes of mood from happy to sad, from consolation to desolation. The belief given to us by Jesus that we are loved and cherished by God one by one – a gift we cannot cancel – makes decision making infinitely more stress free. God's love is what matters, and I cannot lose that treasure even if later I see I made a mistake in my decision.

The man in the story, once healed, wants to get in the boat and go with Jesus, but Jesus asks him to stay home and show his cure to friends and neighbours. For us, if we can come to trust in our new identity as children of God, then it no longer makes a great difference whether we are called by Jesus to work full-time in Christian ministry or simply called by him to live our daily lives in gratitude and peace.

FIVE

Bent double

Luke 13:10-17

There are two things going on in this story. Luke the evangelist is a physician, and he is interested in Jesus curing yet another kind of ailment. In addition to the cure itself, there is a heartless complaint that Jesus has healed someone on the Sabbath day, as if that is more important than the poor woman's affliction. In a mean-spirited way, the complainant picks on the weak one, the woman who had been bent over but now is able to stand straight, and tells her off for allowing herself to be cured on the holy day. He addresses the whole congregation in the synagogue, not just the healed woman. Really he is getting at Jesus, but he does not have the courage to say so outright.

As usual in the Gospel stories of healing, there are two main things for us to learn, 21 centuries after the event. Firstly, we can admire and love the tender way in which Jesus spots the ailment and the ailing one. And then we can work out what the story tells us about ourselves and about ailing people in our own day.

We cannot guarantee to heal someone who is bent double simply by laying our hands on their bent back. But we can observe the way Jesus spots this lady and calls her over to him. He lays his hands upon her and raises her up, knowing full well that the leader of the synagogue is going to be furious with him for 'working' on the Sabbath. Jesus calls on the critics to at least think how they would not fail to water their precious animals on the Sabbath – they have probably done no less that same morning. And Jesus reminds them that this is a daughter of Abraham, their own kin, their own sister, who has been in bondage to Satan for 18 years. Jesus, who elsewhere tells us to come to him and change our burdens for his light one, lifts the burden that has been bending the back of this unhappy woman and sets her free. This is the kind of healer and saviour who is still with us.

What does the story tell us today about ourselves? For one thing, Jesus does not want us to go year after year bent double. When we are overcome with worries, we might as well be bent over, since all we can see is the ground before us and not the beautiful blue sky, not the green trees and the flowers or whatever is of beauty where we live, not the beauty of children and young people, not the love in others' eyes. We cannot count our blessings because we cannot see them: we can only see our own feet.

What makes the difference is the gift of Jesus to know ourselves as sons and daughters of God, with a 'bank balance' in God that is richer than all the silver and gold in the world. I can look the world in the eye and know myself as important as anyone else. This can make a world of difference to someone burdened with anxieties, and it can even make a difference to someone physically burdened and bent. To know that God will love me the same whichever way I choose – that lifts the burden from every anxious choice and leaves me free to use my common sense.

SIX

Feeding the four thousand

Mark 8:1-10

Mark's story of how Jesus fed 4000 people has a very different feel from his account of the feeding of the 5000. With the 4000, the question the disciples ask is, 'How can one feed these people with bread here in the desert?' They are in a desert place, far from habitation. Before, in the story of the 5000, the grass was green, the freshwater lake was nearby and there were villages round about where the people could have gone to buy food for themselves.

For the 5000, Jesus acts as the promised Shepherd, showing compassion and instructing. He makes the people lie down on the green grass by the fresh waters and feeds them all, at no charge, and there is plenty left over. He is giving a living demonstration of the promises in Psalm 23, in Ezekiel and in Isaiah – all fulfilled in himself.

In today's story of the feeding of the 4000, however, Mark is showing Jesus as another Moses, feeding the people in the desert. When long ago Moses was dying, and when it was clear that he himself would never lead the people into the Promised Land, he promised that God would send another like himself, to whom the people would listen. Here in today's story we have Jesus feeding the people in the desert, just as Moses did.

How beautiful and consoling are the words Jesus uses in the desert:

> I have compassion for the crowd, because they have been with me now for three days and have nothing to eat. If I send them away hungry to their homes, they will faint on the way – and some of them have come from a great distance.

These are words that still touch our hearts, centuries afterwards, because Jesus is the same yesterday, today and for ever. He still has compassion on us whenever we have set out to listen to his words. He is still and again aware that we have come a long way for his sake – not just the road to church but years, perhaps decades, which can feel like a very long way at times. He does not want us to faint on the way home, during the later part of our lives as we travel on the way home to God.

When it comes to the Eucharist, in a particular way these words of Jesus can enter deeply into our hearts. This is the manna that keeps us going, that gives us the stamina to get to the other side of any desert we are going through. Whether we are doing well or poorly, Jesus has compassion; he knows how far we have come, and how much the journey has taken out of us. He knows we still have a long way ahead of us, but he will continue to lead us.

Listen to him: these words of Jesus are well worth listening to every single day.

SEVEN

The last word?

Luke 12:8, 9

Jesus sometimes makes statements that sound pretty final, but on other occasions he softens the same statements by relenting and forgiving. Take for instance this saying of Jesus which comes in our Gospel reading for today. He says, 'And I tell you, everyone who acknowledges me before others, the Son of Man also will acknowledge before the angels of God; but whoever denies me before others will be denied before the angels of God.'

That sounds fairly universal, applying as it does to 'everyone'. But if we pause and think, we can come up with some famous exceptions. Most of the apostles chose to run away rather than acknowledge Jesus when he was arrested. Peter did not run away, but his denials were spectacular: warming himself at the fire, he managed to deny Jesus in front of the maid and the soldiers three times. He denied that he ever knew the man, even cursing and swearing when it came to the third time.

Yet Jesus did not deny Peter before the angels of God. On the contrary, he forgave him and confirmed his place among the apostles, as we learn from John's Gospel (John 20). Most likely, too, when Luke tells us 'the Lord turned and looked at Peter' just after Peter's denials (Luke 22:61), that was the moment Peter realised what he had just done, and was heartbroken.

In this context of Jesus making exceptions to his own rules, it would be good to remember the thief on the cross beside Jesus, to whom Jesus promises Paradise that same day (Luke 23:39-43). As we know from Matthew, Jesus puts in pride of place the feeding of the hungry, giving drink to the thirsty, clothing the naked, welcoming the stranger, visiting the sick, visiting the prisoners (Matthew 25:31-46). Yet here on the next cross is a dying thief who has spent his career taking the food from others, taking the clothes off their backs, targeting strangers, making healthy people feel sick at heart. Probably the only prison visiting he ever did was when he was committed to prison himself. In the matter of the king separating the sheep from the goats, this man is surely on the side of the goats. Yet because he does not judge Jesus, but believes in him, and because he asks Jesus to remember him when he comes into his kingdom, all is forgiven. The thief joins the sheep.

For our own consolation, we need to remember that Jesus, putting words into the mouth of the judging king, only condemns those who *never* in their lives did a work of kindness or mercy. Even the thief had a kind word to say to Jesus on the cross.

EIGHT

Birds, rock, thorns, good soil

Mark 4:1-20

We have heard today the start of Jesus' programme of parables spoken from the boat to the crowds on the shore. He tells the story about the sower who went out to sow and about the fate of the different seeds, depending on what kind of terrain they fell upon. Some were eaten by the birds because they fell exposed on the path; some fell on rocky ground; some fell among thorns and thistles, and the plant that grew was choked; others fell on good ground, and produced good, better and best crops.

Then, says Mark, those who are around Jesus with the 12 are given an explanation of the parable. As the explanation is written, it might seem to be describing four different types of people, doomed to the fate of being gobbled up swiftly by birds, withering on rocky ground, being choked by thorns and thistles, or else (the good ones) producing thirty, sixty or a hundredfold of the crop. The listener might be excused for asking, 'Which one am I? How can I avoid ending up among the seeds that produce nothing useful? Is Jesus looking at me when he talks about the birds, the rocky ground, the thorns?'

Jesus also tells his close companions that unless they understand this parable, they are not likely to understand any of the parables. Helpfully, for readers of Mark's Gospel, the understanding comes to light as the story progresses. Peter is the example of having the word snatched from him; James and John are on rocky ground; all the 12 are bewitched by riches. Yet these are the apostles who end up most fruitful, in a way that is still producing fruit 21 centuries later.

Peter has just received the word from God about Jesus being the Christ, but the next minute he is trying to stop Jesus from going to Jerusalem, and Jesus is saying to him, 'Get behind me, Satan' (Matthew 16:23), equating Peter to the first category of the seed parable: the birds come – 'Satan immediately comes and takes away the word that is sown in them' (Mark 4:15). Then James and John are full of zeal and thunder, but when Jesus is arrested they run away. All the disciples travelling to Jerusalem with Jesus are astounded when he teaches them that earthly riches are not so much a blessing as a burden (Mark 10:23-31).

Mark gives clear indications that the three categories are found among the apostles, and so there must be stages a disciple goes through rather than fixed states we cannot get out of.

As for the thirtyfold, sixtyfold and a hundredfold, it is worth recalling that a humble dandelion produces nearly 100 little parachutes; a duck produces only seven or eight ducklings. Each creature has its optimum, so 100 is not necessarily the best.

NINE

'Come to me . . .'

Matthew 11:25-30

Many years ago, when I was first coming to grips with the four Gospels, I attended some lectures by a German biblical scholar on the Gospel according to Matthew. One thing above all I remember with gratitude from his talks: he said that these few lines in Matthew, quoting Jesus, are the title of the book, the heart of the Gospel and the key to the whole message.

> Come to me, all you that are weary and are carrying heavy burdens, and I will give you rest. Take my yoke upon you, and learn from me; for I am gentle and humble in heart, and you will find rest for your souls. For my yoke is easy, and my burden is light.

How the lecturer came to the conclusion that this short saying of Jesus was the key to the whole Gospel of Matthew went like this: in the Gospel there are five major themes, with five important discourses – one to go with each theme. First comes the Sermon on the Mount, then the instructions for the disciples being sent on mission, next comes the mystery of the kingdom, then the shape of the Church, then the universal nature of the Church.

Matthew, being a Jewish writer, is using a Jewish style of writing whereby the most important passage is in the middle, not at the beginning or end. Think 3, 2, 1, 2, 3 – the middle finger of my hand is the important one; not my thumb, not my little finger. And among those five stages of Matthew's Gospel, in the middle of the one in the middle is our Gospel passage for today: Jesus says, 'Come to me.'

That saying of Jesus, the lecturer told us, is the clearest statement in the whole Gospel asserting the divinity of Jesus. Who else could stand up and cry to the whole world, 'If your burdens are heavy, come to me, whoever you are, wherever you are, now or in the future. My yoke is easy, so do not be afraid to take it on you. Here you will find rest for your souls.'

If these words, so gentle and sympathetic and helpful, are the key to the rest of Matthew's Gospel, then we should surely work out the meaning of the rest by comparing the rest with the key, so as to gain understanding. Other stories and commands in the Gospel may at first strike us as sombre or difficult or even impossible, but then we must have misunderstood them. The burdens we already carry are heavier than the yoke Jesus volunteers to share with us, so why not drop them and take up his friendly offer? Everything else then falls into place.

TEN

Martha and Mary

Luke 10:38-42

'Now as they went on their way, he entered a certain village . . .' That is the story of long ago, but as usual with the Gospel stories there is a 'then' and a 'now'. There is what Jesus said and did then, and there is a lesson along the same lines to be listened for and listened to today.

On a personal note, what jolted me first about this story happened when I was reading the passage in Latin, in the Vulgate translation of St Jerome. For 'he entered a certain village', the Latin read *intravit quoddam castellum*, which sounded to me like 'he entered a certain castle', and I immediately thought of how our inner life is often compared to an interior castle. Anyway, at that moment it was as if Jesus had entered my interior castle. Then he entered a certain village; now he was entering my heart.

What happened in the house of Martha and Mary has a personal message for the reader even today. First of all, it is a tremendous honour that Jesus comes to stay in your heart or in my heart. There is a presence of Jesus in the Eucharist, but now and again we can be vividly aware that Jesus is present in the Gospel story, speaking intimately to me the reader or the hearer.

What is going on between Jesus and Martha and Mary in the story has clear echoes in the lives of most Christians a lot of the time. For 'Mary' read the desire to pray, the yearning for a contemplative life. For 'Martha' read the roller coaster of work that we feel should be done, but it leaves not enough time for prayer. What must Jesus be saying, in our 'interior castle'? It is clear from the original story that Jesus leans in the direction of Mary's choice in this instance. Martha has decided that her way is the right way, and everything she is planning for her guest is necessary. Jesus himself has a different scale of values.

My guess is that Mary would not see sitting at the feet of Jesus and listening to him as the be all and end all of the day. She is making sure she hears Jesus aright – what he wants, what he does not want – then she will get up and follow the track he has set out, confident that she goes with his blessing. We today do not have that same joy of physically sitting at Jesus' feet, but we can present to ourselves the alternatives before us and sense which choice will bring us his peace, and in that way go forward with Jesus.

Martha, with the best will in the world, has made preparations for Jesus without asking him what he really wants. We, too, can rush into things, only to find that they do not work, or else that they are doing us more harm than good. But we can learn from our past experience and find the right balance between prayer and action.

ELEVEN

Jesus' baptism and mine

Mark 1:9-11; Matthew 3:13-15

Imagine, if you will, that you are a friend of Jesus in Nazareth before he becomes famous. Jesus decides to go down and see what John the Baptist is doing – John who is to prepare the way for Jesus' own public life. John is baptising people in the River Jordan while they ask for the forgiveness of their sins.

Imagine that you and a few other young people decide to go with Jesus to see what is happening. Jesus shuts up the carpenter's shop and says au revoir to his mother Mary, and the company of walkers sets out. How long or how short is the journey? Over hills or down valleys? Good roads or bad tracks? Camping nights or staying at inns? Imagine it whatever way you wish; the main point is that you are in the company of Jesus. You come to the place on the River Jordan where John is baptising. There is a bit of a carnival atmosphere, an air of happiness. Jesus and you join the queue, waiting for John to take each person into the water. 'Are you willing to admit you are a sinner?' asks John, and, 'Do you admit that you need God's help and forgiveness?' If the answer is yes, John lowers the person into the water.

John sees Jesus in the line of people waiting and wants to exchange places: Jesus should be the one to do the baptisms. Jesus says no, to leave things as they are. He wishes to be at one with the ordinary people. Then Jesus is baptised. Just as he is coming up out of the water, he sees the heavens torn apart (nothing between him and God) and the Spirit descending on him like a dove. And a voice comes from heaven: 'You are my Son, the Beloved; with you I am well pleased.'

Now imagine that Jesus comes out, dripping wet, and says to you, 'You next! I want you to experience what I have just experienced.' So in you go, admitting to be a sinner in need of help.

As you come up out of the water, you see the heavens torn apart, nothing between God and you. The Spirit comes on you, in you, like a dove, like the dove that brought the olive branch to Noah in the ark. The Spirit brings the promise of peace, of forgiveness, of reconciliation. The voice from heaven says to you, 'You are my son, the beloved; with you I am well pleased,' or, 'You are my daughter, the beloved; with you I am well pleased.'

You say, 'How can you be well pleased with me, a sinner?'

And the voice from heaven replies, 'I am pleased with you not because you are a sinner but because you are mine, my child. My favour rests on you and does not go away. You are as much my favourite as anyone else alive.'

As you come out, Jesus welcomes you as his beloved younger sister, his beloved younger brother.

Does this picture of being baptised along with Jesus seem too good to be true? Or is it perhaps not a true way to understand Christian baptism?

TWELVE

Transfiguration

Matthew 17:1-8

The transfiguration of Jesus is a many-splendoured event, with layers and layers of meaning. Jesus is revealed to Peter, to James and to John as the beloved Son of God with whom God is well pleased. Jesus speaks familiarly with Moses and with Elijah who represent the Law and the Prophets; then Moses and Elijah depart, pointing to Jesus as the fulfilment of the Law and the Prophets.

As they are there on the mountain, a bright cloud suddenly covers them – the Spirit like a cloud now, rather than a dove as before. And the voice from the cloud speaks to the three disciples and says, 'This is my Son, the Beloved; with him I am well pleased; listen to him!' Jesus is thus named as the same who was baptised by John. Furthermore, Jesus is named as the one promised from long ago who would take the place of Moses when Moses should die, the one who was to be listened to: 'you shall heed such a prophet' (Deuteronomy 18:15).

Jesus' baptism is not something he clings to for himself only: he has shared it with all of us, making us his brothers and sisters. He wanted, and still wants, the whole world to be baptised and to know their dignity as children of the good God. What about his transfiguration? Is that for himself alone, or is there something else in our own lives that he wishes to share with us? I think there is. We do it without always making the connection with the transfiguration.

Imagine yourself to be one of the three – Peter, James or John – or else you could be a fourth disciple going up the mountain with Jesus. Jesus' face begins to shine like the sun, and his clothes become dazzling white. After his conversation with Moses and Elijah comes the bright and fearful cloud, and the voice of the Father from the cloud.

Imagine that Jesus stands you next to him to hear the words from the cloud: 'This is my daughter, my son, the beloved; with her, with him, I am well pleased; listen to her, listen to him!' You are still beloved: nothing can destroy your baptism. But now you are to be listened to, as Jesus was.

What are you to say for people to listen to? Simply this: that you are God's beloved child even though you are far from perfect, and that this

Psalm 67

1 God be gracious to us and bless us •
   and make his face to shine upon us,

2 That your way may be known upon earth, •
   your saving power among all nations.

3 Let the peoples praise you, O God; •
   let all the peoples praise you.

4 O let the nations rejoice and be glad, •
   for you will judge the peoples righteously
      and govern the nations upon earth.

5 Let the peoples praise you, O God; •
   let all the peoples praise you.

6 Then shall the earth bring forth her increase, •
   and God, our own God, will bless us.

7 God will bless us, •
   and all the ends of the earth shall fear him.

Glory to the Father and to the Son and to the Holy Spirit; as it was in the beginning is now and shall be for ever.
Amen

same gift is on offer to anyone who is listening. Where Jesus had to be listened to was at his trial, when the high priest asked him whether he was the Messiah, the Son of God (Matthew 26:63). Jesus gave the answer, but he was not listened to. The simple answer you are to give will not please everyone either.

What it comes to, surely, is that in our baptism we recognise ourselves as children of God, and that instinctively we need to follow up the baptism with a life of gratitude and service. In most Christian denominations there follows a ceremony of confirmation, whether as infants, as children, as teenagers or as adults. This is not to celebrate our own commitment, since we (along with Peter, James and John) cannot guarantee to be faithful. What we celebrate is the fact that God will never stop calling us, even though we fail so often to respond.

THIRTEEN

'Abba!'

Luke 11:2; Mark 14:35

A friend of mine by the name of Tony told me this story. He was on a two-week trip to the Holy Land, and one day instead of being a pilgrim he spent a day by the seaside, beside the Mediterranean. Sunshine does not bother him, so he was in a deckchair, reading peacefully. He noticed some yards in front of him a little Jewish boy intently creating a sandcastle. When the castle was completed to the little lad's satisfaction, he ran over to his Daddy who was reclining in another deckchair nearby and called him to come and admire the castle. *'Abba! Abba!'* was what he said, gesturing to please come and see.

My friend Tony was brought up short. Here, in the land of Jesus, was a little child using the same word for his father that Jesus used when speaking to his Father – the word, the name, moreover, that Jesus wants *us* to use when speaking to God. Not just the name, but the whole relationship was made clear to Tony there by the seaside. Your *Abba* is someone who will be interested in a sandcastle you have just made; your heavenly *Abba* has time to spare for you. God as *Abba* wants you to become like a little child, lovingly, trustingly bringing every matter, great or small, to the Father's attention.

All of this had a special significance for Tony. He was a priest and had recently been asked by his bishop to take charge of updating the schools' religious syllabus in the diocese. The little boy and his sandcastle became a standard against which to review each year of the religious programme: instead of the policeman/judge/lawyer image of God that kept cropping up in the previous syllabus, there would be a constant matching up with the *Abba* image.

It helps to remember always that there are two versions of the Lord's Prayer: one in Matthew's Gospel and one in Luke. Matthew's version starts in what is for us the familiar way: 'Our Father . . .' (Matthew 6:9). Luke starts simply, 'Father' – that is to say, *Abba*, in the same way as Jesus prayed in the garden before his arrest. It must have been the word *Abba* that Luke was translating: there is no other hidden name that Jesus would have used. When I pray on my own, I may call God '*Abba*, my Father'. When we pray along with other Christians, we pray 'Our Father, our *Abba*'.

There is a great blessing in being allowed by Luke's Gospel (as also by Paul in his letters) to call God my Father. Even if by some sad chance I should ever come adrift from the rest of the Church, I may still call upon God as my very own *Abba*! Through my baptism I have my own place at God's table, which no one can take from me. My relationship with God is unique; his family is not complete until all of us are home, and that includes the least one, the lost sheep, who could one day be me.

FOURTEEN

Clean

Leviticus 15:19-30; Mark 5:24-34

Today's Gospel story is a tale within a tale. Jesus is on his way to the house of Jairus, where Jairus' little girl lies dying; crowds are flocking round Jesus and the father of the girl. A woman in the crowd elbows her way towards Jesus and touches his cloak from behind. For 12 years she has been plagued with non-stop haemorrhages; she has spent all she had on physicians, has 'endured much' under them, and is no better, but rather worse.

The social implications of this ailment were enormous and distressing. According to the Book of Leviticus, a woman haemorrhaging was ritually unclean. She would make unclean anything or anybody she touched, and anybody or anything that touched her. This would perhaps be bearable for a day or two at a time, but to have it for 12 years without remission?! The poor woman must have had a miserable life, and must have been thoroughly frustrated.

Now she hears about Jesus and his powers of healing. She wants to come to him, in spite of the crowds around him. She wants to touch his cloak – an action which in the ordinary way would make Jesus unclean until the evening, but she believes his goodness is stronger than any uncleanness. Recklessly she elbows her way through the crowd; it no longer worries her that she is rendering unclean half the population of the town. She struggles on until she is behind Jesus, and she touches his cloak. Immediately she feels herself to be healed; and when Jesus asks who it was that touched his clothes, she knows what he means and owns up.

Then Jesus says to her, 'Daughter, your faith has made you well; go in peace, and be healed of your disease.' The woman is not the daughter of Jesus, but she is the beloved daughter of God. There is a dignity infinitely above ordinary human life: no one is to be called unclean who is good enough to be called 'my beloved daughter' by God the Holy One.

As is usual with healing stories from the Gospels, there are at least two ways to understand them and to apply them to ourselves. The first is the way of admiration, taking in the details of the story and marvelling at the power of Jesus to heal the person or persons involved.

The second way to take a healing story to ourselves is to identify in imagination with the person being healed by Jesus. Am I ever shunned by other individuals or groups of people as if I were unclean? Am I afflicted by any sickness or disfigurement that makes people leave me severely alone? Do I live on the wrong side of the railway tracks, where the less desirable folk are to be found?

That is where the story in today's Gospel reading can come in. As far as Jesus is concerned (and he is the truth), I am not unclean; I am God's beloved daughter or God's beloved son, and I can cling to this truth in my heart, no matter what anybody says.

FIFTEEN

The promised Shepherd

Mark 6:30-52

Mark tells us that the apostles rowing away in the boat do not understand about the loaves (verse 52); they do not gather the real significance of Jesus' feeding of the 5000. Yet, as retold by Mark, the meaning comes across clearly to us.

Jesus intended to take the apostles away to a lonely place, to rest and to digest what they have experienced in their first mission work. Instead, they come ashore to thousands of people hungry to hear what Jesus has to say to them. Instead of being cross, or sailing away again, Jesus has compassion on the crowd, because they are 'like sheep without a shepherd' (verse 34). The prophet Ezekiel described the kind of Shepherd God was promising (Ezekiel 34:11-24): looking for the lost, bringing back the strayed, binding up the injured, strengthening the weak. He would take away the sheep from their regular shepherds, who were feeding themselves at the expense of the sheep; from now on God himself would feed them; his son David, the chosen Shepherd himself, would feed them. In Jesus this is already happening: Jesus is leaving aside the synagogues for the hillsides and the open country, and the hungry sheep are following him, the Son of David. First he gives them food for the mind and heart – he speaks to them with compassion.

When the time comes to feed them with bread, Jesus makes them lie down on the green grass (verse 39). Usually translators say that he made them 'sit down', but the word Mark uses is the same as the Greek word for the sheep to 'lie down' that is used in Ezekiel 34:14 and Psalm 23:2. The Shepherd makes the sheep to lie down on the green grass. They are beside the fresh waters of the lake. This is a deserted or lonely place, but it is not a desert like the place where 4000 were fed. Here there are villages nearby, where food might be obtained; here the grass is green.

Jesus tells the apostles to divide the people into groups. That would leave green grassy pathways between each group for the apostles to circulate. Mark uses a strange expression to describe the scene: the people were divided up 'flowerbeds, flowerbeds' (verse 40, *prasiai prasiai*), and indeed from a distance they must have looked like colourful flowerbeds.

The food should have cost some hundreds of pounds sterling by today's reckoning, but it was free, and given freely. And there was plenty of food left over. If one of us had been at the end of the line in the group furthest away from Jesus, we might well have wondered whether the bread and fish would last as far as me, as far as us. But it did.

In spite of all the signs in the scene relating to Jesus as the promised Shepherd, the disciples leaving the scene seem to be thinking more about destroying the empire of the Romans than about the coming of the kingdom of God. Jesus tells them to take to the boat and leave. When the rowing is hard, and Jesus comes to them over the water, they think it is a ghost. So he tells them, 'Take heart, it is I; do not be afraid.' Their hearts are hardened, says Mark; they do not yet know who he is (verse 52) – but Mark does, and so do we.

SIXTEEN

If it were possible

Mark 14:35

Supposing I have a friend, a friend I turn to in times of need or difficulty. Along comes a difficulty – quite a serious one – and I cannot solve it myself. I think my friend could sort out my problem, so I go to him or her for help. 'For friendship's sake, can you get me out of this fix?' If the answer is 'Yes,' that is usually the end of the problem. But what if the answer is 'No, I cannot do what you ask'?

In that case, there are two thoughts open to me: either my friend is not really my friend after all, or else my friend genuinely cannot find any solution for me in the present situation. If possible, when possible, the friend would willingly come to the rescue.

Now supposing we apply this imaginary scenario to the way we ask God for things. 'Please, God, you say you are my friend; you say you love me. I am in trouble, deep trouble. You are almighty, all powerful, you can do all things. Please get me out of this terrible situation.' Suppose the answer is 'Yes,' then peace of mind returns and I duly give thanks for rescue.

But suppose the answer seems to be 'No'. What then? Seemingly, God could save me but chooses not to. Does that mean God doesn't love me any more? Is a God like that really worth worshipping? Or could it be that God would dearly love to be able to answer my prayer but it is just not possible? It is not possible here and now, regardless of the future or about a solution in eternal life.

Jesus himself more than once said that with God all things are possible. God can see the way to getting a rich man into heaven, or a camel through the eye of a needle. But when it came to Jesus' praying for three hours in the garden just before his arrest, Mark's Gospel tells how he 'threw himself on the ground and prayed that, if it were possible, the hour might pass from him'. *If it were possible*. But it was not possible. Either God was no longer Jesus' beloved *Abba*, or else his *Abba* was unable to rescue Jesus there and then.

Jesus had to continue believing that he was God's beloved Son, and at the same time believe that God his *Abba*, his Father, would rescue him when it became possible. In the meantime, there was no way round the Passion; only the way through the Passion, till the resurrection. So, too, with us in our own sorrows and tribulations; there is often no way round them; only the way through them. We can pray, but like Jesus we have to cling to God's love and beg for help to bring us through our ordeals.

If we believe that God is a loving friend, I think we have to reconsider what we mean by God being all powerful. All powerful in the end, yes; victor over disease, hatred and war; but not always able to magic away our sorrows just because we ask, here and now.

SEVENTEEN

Jesus: the hidden years

Luke 3:23

'Jesus was about thirty years old when he began his work.' We cannot help wondering what Jesus was like before he began his work of preaching and teaching. What was he like as a little boy? As a 10-year-old? We know something important about him at the age of 12, when he went missing from his parents and was found after three days in the temple. But then, what was he like as a teenager; what was he like in his 20s? We are told very little about these years in Jesus' life, so what kind of guesswork can we safely employ?

Classic oil paintings of Jesus as an infant in his mother's arms tend to be unrealistic, even though they may be very beautiful. My own favourite is one very realistic scene: it is called *The Madonna of the Basket* by Correggio, an oil painting that now hangs in the National Gallery in London. Mary has just finished knitting a cardigan for 2-year-old Jesus who is sitting on her lap. The remains of the knitting wool is in the basket at Mary's feet. Little Jesus is trying to be helpful, struggling to get both arms into the cardigan to see if it is a good fit. Mary is not just smiling at his efforts; she has a big grin on her face. In the background is Joseph, sawing a plank and missing the fun. The artist sees, and we can see, the little fellow is stretching out his arms in the form of a cross.

Pictures of the family's flight into Egypt are many and varied, and some depict an imaginary rest on the journey, with Joseph gathering fruit for them to eat. Here my favourite is one by Rembrandt, where they are not at rest but are in the dark of night, moving as far away from Herod as fast as possible. Joseph's drill can be seen in the pack on the donkey's back – he will need to earn a living.

The apocryphal gospels have some wild and wonderful made-up tales about Jesus' childhood. One example tells of the time the other children in Nazareth would not let Jesus play with them, so he turned them all into little pigs.[1] When their mothers appealed to Mary she made Jesus turn them back into little people! Another tale has Joseph

---

1. The Gospel of Thomas, from Montague Rhodes James (trans), *The Apocryphal New Testament*, Oxford, at the Clarendon Press, 1955.

sawing off a plank too short. Young Jesus said not to worry, 'You hold one end, Joseph, and I'll pull on the other end till it's the right length again!'[2]

Certain it is, though, that Jesus did have an apprenticeship as a carpenter. Also we can only marvel at the original stories and teaching he used so skilfully once he reached the age of 30. He must for years have been extremely observant of all that went on in the fields and in the towns and in the city, and he must have been making up his parables as the years went by, storing them for future use. Commentators on the Gospels have noticed that many of Jesus' sayings are in fact Hebrew-style poems – they are not impromptu words thrown together; they are poems lovingly created and remembered from back in the hidden years when he created them.

---

2. Ibid.

EIGHTEEN

Weeds among the wheat

Matthew 13:24-30

There are different ways of understanding this parable of Jesus. At first sight it seems to imply that some people are good and will remain good all their lives, whereas some others are evil and will remain evil to the end. Jesus would hardly have meant us to understand the parable so, since the story gives no space for the weeds to turn into wheat. All Jesus' other stories make room for conversion of heart to happen in our lifetime, but here the good and the bad are fixed from start to finish.

How, then, to understand the parable better? The easiest way is for the reader or the listener to say, 'That field is me; it reminds me of me. I set out with the best of intentions to please God, but my life is full of faults. The good I mean to do does not get done; wrong things I never meant to do – those I do. I feel like the good field with weeds among the wheat, weeds that I dearly wish were not there.'

What, then, to do about the situation? I would like to pull out all the weeds, yet Jesus' parable makes me pause. He seems to be telling me not to concentrate on removing the weeds but to concentrate on whatever is good.

I have a story from my own life that illustrates the greater value of staying with the good. I was in teacher training and was observing a teacher with a class of 10-year-olds. It was the half-hour in the afternoon given over to personal time for reading storybooks. To my amazement the teacher spent a full quarter of an hour telling the children off because they did not read enough. It was a classic case of concentrating on the faults and well-nigh destroying the good. The whole class, including me as the observer, felt disheartened.

After that, I was determined to go easy on the red pencil when my turn came to be marking exercises. A page full of red crosses is enough to dampen the enthusiasm of the best of youngsters, whereas encouraging the good parts can lead to good results much more quickly.

Looked at in this light, the parable is motivating us to concentrate not on our faults but on any good that we can do. The message is similar to the way Jesus cures the paralysed man by telling him his sins are forgiven (Mark 2:5). No need to lie there lamenting over the weaknesses of the past; rather, get up and do something. We will probably have our faults and weaknesses for the rest of our lives; but in the resurrection the good field of wheat will be there, but the weeds will all be gone.

There is a similar lesson to be learned, and it goes like this. Saying thank you to God is more powerful than any number of complaints, and remembering to give thanks has a cheerful and positive effect on the human spirit. For wheat, think thanks; for weeds, think complaints.

NINETEEN

Even better than being good

Luke 15:11-32

I want to talk about the elder brother. The elder brother had been doing more than his share of the work in the field for years, obeying faithfully his instructions as to what was to be done. Result: no thanks from his father; no young goat ever to celebrate with his friends. Yet when the brother we call the prodigal comes home, in disgrace really, there is music and dancing, the fatted calf is killed for a banquet, a ring is placed on his finger and the best robe put on his back. Naturally the elder brother is dismayed, and finds himself unwilling to join in the festivities.

Naturally, yes. Jesus in this story is telling us that there is something even more important than the faithful performance of duties, and that is the forgiveness of the sinner. Jesus is not saying that duty does not matter: he wants us to be faithful to our duties all our lives, but also to be forgiving towards those who make a wreck of their lives. That is not 'natural' to us, but it is according to God's way of thinking.

Life, in God's eyes, is not a simple matter of doing the right thing all our days and then being welcomed into heaven when we die. We need to realise that doing the right thing all our days is a gift from God, and not something we can pat ourselves on the back for. The lives of the saints give glory to God, not to the saints themselves.

A parallel story is the one told by Jesus about the two men who went to pray in the temple – the Pharisee and the tax collector (Luke 18:10-14). The Pharisee congratulated himself at having fasted when he should, given alms when he should, prayed when he should. He stood up at the front of the shrine with nothing to be afraid of before God. He prided himself on being worlds better than the tax collector. The tax collector, on the other hand, kept his eyes down, stood at the back of the shrine and asked God to be merciful to him, sinner as he was. He said nothing against the Pharisee.

Jesus reckoned it was the tax collector who went away justified. The Pharisee was taking to himself what was really a gift of God. The tax collector was admitting his own helplessness to do good without the grace of God.

In a similar way, Jesus' story of the prodigal son and the elder brother favours the returned sinner over the hard-working but hard-hearted stay-at-home. We need God's grace not only to be faithful year after year, but also to forgive those who have been unfaithful. Jesus himself is our elder brother, the firstborn in the new creation, and we are all his younger brothers and sisters. Thanks be to God that our brother Jesus is what the one in this story should have been: he worked for our good every moment of his life, but he did not come to condemn, only to forgive. He had only one plan, one wish, with his heavenly Father: forgiveness.

TWENTY

Nothingness blessed

Luke 1:46-55

There is a lovely old English poem by Thomas Traherne, called 'The Salutation'. The poet imagines a baby boy lying there admiring his fingers and toes, his feelings and joys, all the things that go with being alive in a beautiful world. And yet, the baby muses, until a year or two ago none of that was there. 'I came out of nowhere, from nothing to something wonderful' is more or less the theme of the poem.

Mary the expectant mother of Jesus has the same awareness: 'for he has looked in favour on the lowliness of his servant. Surely, from now on all generations will call me blessed.' He has looked on his servant in her nothingness. 'I am a nothing called into life by God; I am a nothing greatly blessed by God.' God raises the lowly up high, those who understand that they are nothing in themselves.

The proud-hearted, on the other hand, who think that anything good they have done was done all by themselves, have a big disappointment to come when they realise their power was a gift all along, a gift that could be withdrawn.

Luke in his Gospel credits Mary with this great wisdom, shown in her poem we call the *Magnificat.* Matthew in his Gospel has a story told by Jesus that amounts to the same thing: a story about the labourers in the vineyard (Matthew 20:1-16). You remember how it goes: the owner of the vineyard takes on casual labourers at different hours of the day, such that some work all the day, some a half-day, and some only the final hour of the day. When he pays their wages he gives all of them the same amount, a fair wage for a day's work – even though some of them had by no means worked all day. Somebody complains.

The landowner is not impressed by the complainer. 'Am I not allowed to do what I choose with what belongs to me? Or are you envious because I am generous?' Those who worked all day receive the just wage they agreed. For the others, it is not their fault that they were unable to do a full day's work: it was not within their power to do more, because no one hired them.

What this is adding up to is that those who worked all day stood in their nothingness to begin with, and were given the gift of the chance to work. The hard-working people who find work find it as a gift. If they begin to think this belongs to them, they are in for a land, a disappointment. If they think badly of those who are only able to work less, they have forgotten who is the owner of their days. They had better take their wages and go.

Surely we will find there is only one heaven, and we will be blessed to find ourselves there, without totting up whether everyone else has earned eternal happiness. Nobody could ever earn that.

TWENTY-ONE

How many times?

Matthew 18:21, 22

Peter seems to be having some difficulty keeping up with Jesus. All this about forgiveness is beginning to feel somewhat limitless. So Peter tries to put a reasonable cap on the number of times he can be expected to forgive one of the brethren who offends him. How about seven times? Would that be enough? There was a popular recognition that even a good person falls seven times in the day, so that would mean reinstating a good person at the end of each day. Peter does not seem to be asking about how many times to forgive an enemy.

There was a telling scene in a popular old film that shows Peter having problems forgiving. *Jesus of Nazareth* was the film, Franco Zeffirelli the director. Jesus has just called Matthew the tax collector to join his followers. Peter was not there on that occasion, so when Peter returns to the gathering he is startled to see Matthew sitting with Jesus: Matthew the tax collector, the sinner, the customs clerk who is no friend to fisherfolk. Dilemma for Peter: does he stay with Jesus or does he go off in a huff, thinking, 'This is too much'? He decides to stay.

Jesus' answer to the question of how many times to forgive is all-embracing: we should forgive 77 times. I think, balancing his reply with Peter's question, that Jesus means 77 times in a day. Other manuscripts telling of this exchange have Jesus saying '70 x 7 times' or 490 times, which is a lot of forgiveness, whether in a day, a year or a lifetime. Pretty obviously, Jesus is saying, 'Forgive every time.'

All this is about our forgiving one another and about forgiving our enemies, and that is a very difficult teaching on Jesus' part. The Gospels tell us that Jesus himself asked his Father – it was almost his dying wish – to forgive those who were crucifying him, on the unlikely grounds that they did not know what they were doing. Jesus did not fail to do what he asks of us. Stephen the first martyr, as his dying wish, asked Jesus in heaven to forgive those who were stoning him to death.

But there is another side to these figures, these 77s, and it is this: God will forgive us at least 77 times, every time we fall and fail. God will never get tired of forgiving. God would not ask us to do something above and beyond what he himself is ready to do.

We humans have a fear that if we turn our backs on God and run away, then every step we take will have to be retraced towards God before we can be forgiven. In fact, all we have to do is to turn round on the spot, wherever we have reached in our flight.

Turn round and see that God never changed, never shut us out of the light, never stopped being welcoming. All is well instantly, and with God's help we can then begin to put things right.

TWENTY-TWO

No fixed abode

Luke 9:57, 58

I worked out once that for Jesus there are three kinds of poverty. There is the most complete kind of poverty, whereby the generous person gives everything to the poor then lives on charity, as Jesus did himself. Then there is what might be called spiritual poverty, by which a generous person sits lightly to all his or her possessions and to all the precious goods of this world – let them come, let them go, God's love is still there. The third kind of poverty I call poverty of merit, whereby followers of Jesus do not add up the merits they think they have gained, nor compare them with merits gained by others. This third kind may seem irrelevant, but I think it is very important in Jesus' eyes.

The first kind of poverty can only really work for a limited number of believers in any one community of Christians. If everybody sold all their goods and gave the money to the poor, there would be no one left to be charitable towards the penniless ones. This, it seems, happened to the infant Christian Church in Jerusalem (Acts 4:32-5). As a result we find Paul fund-raising among the Corinthians after a successful appeal among the Macedonians. Jesus himself was able to live his flexible way of life only because of certain women who provided for him out of their own means. He had no place of his own to lay his head, but he trusted himself to Providence and to the goodness of his followers.

The second kind of poverty is within the reach of everybody. It creates a community that is willing to lend and to borrow, to share and care for one another. I love the little old poem of William Blake – he calls it 'Eternity':

> He who binds to himself a joy
> does the wingèd life destroy.
> He who kisses a joy as it flies
> lives in Eternity's sunrise.[3]

Everything beautiful in the world is free so long as we do not try to pin it down and say, 'This is mine, not yours.' I might catch a butterfly and pin it down in my collection, but then the butterfly is dead, no longer in flight in the sunlight.

3. William Blake (1757–1827), 'Eternity'.

In this detached form of poverty we can all approximate to the freedom of Jesus. Like the old American song title, 'Wherever I lay my hat, that's my home.'[4] Home is when I am with God, and that is not tied to one particular roof. I can be happy wherever I find myself. I can manage with whatever goods or companions come my way, just like the birds of the air, or the flowers.

The third kind of poverty matters to Jesus. He wants our left hand not to know what our right hand is doing. If we add up our virtues and good works and rely on them for salvation, then we will either be proud if we seem to be doing all right or despondent because we are not doing as well as some others. Considering that virtues are a gift of God, it seems best not to be counting them at all.

---

4. 'Wherever I lay my hat, that's my home', written by Marvin Gaye, Barrett Strong and Norman Whitfield, first recorded by Marvin Gaye in 1962.

TWENTY-THREE

'Do not judge . . .'

Luke 6:37

This little group of sayings of Jesus is not always seen as a charter of freedom, but that is what it is: enormous good news. 'Do not judge . . . do not condemn . . . Forgive . . .' The net result is God will not judge me; God will not condemn me; God will forgive me. If this is my settled intention, then I need not be anxious about the mistakes I make that others judge me for: I am forgiven as I go along by the One that matters, and I can start all over again after every slip.

Human nature being what it is, we are inclined to judge other people instantly and instinctively. There is usually a need to stop and to say to myself, 'I do not want to be judged, so I immediately withdraw the charges I was making against this person.' In other words, shake free of the judgement, drop the charges, take off the judge's wig and gown, and become free again.

Lawyers, judges, teachers and parents are all expected to make judgements by the very fact of being who they are. They are all trained to put their charges right. But there is a huge difference between judging that a rule has been broken and saying that the lawbreaker is a wicked, evil person. Who knows what goes on in the mind and heart of another person? Jesus himself made excuses for the people who were crucifying him, and taught his disciples to do the same.

There is something else that Jesus may not necessarily have meant about not judging, but it still fits: 'Do not judge God; do not condemn your Father; do not blame God. Presume that God is loving and well disposed towards you no matter what is happening in your life. Presume that God will get you out of the present predicament as and when it becomes possible. Jesus' prayer in the garden was no less loving because of the terrible circumstances.

In Luke's powerful little list there is a fourth item: Do not judge; do not condemn; forgive . . . and give. In the context with the other three, what we are to give is first and foremost forgiveness rather than money or tangible goods. Give forgiveness and the benefits to yourself will be way beyond anything you expect.

Jesus elsewhere tells us to gather riches that the moths cannot get at (Matthew 6:19). There can be no safer bank than the one that results from not judging other people. Not only does it mean no judgement when we die, but it also means that every day of our lives is free from panic about the mistakes we make. Every day then becomes a new day.

It means there is no longer a sword hanging over our head, waiting for the day of reckoning. It means no longer having to make up a defence for every dubious act we ever did. The 'good thief' on the cross beside Jesus did not try to justify his lifestyle, but he did not judge Jesus; he defended Jesus – and was promised Paradise that same day (Luke 23:39-43).

TWENTY-FOUR

Alexander the coppersmith

2 Timothy 4:14, 15

You may be wondering, 'Who was Alexander the coppersmith?' and 'How does he merit a title all to himself?' The writer of this second letter to Timothy may not have been Paul himself – or so some scholars tell us – but even so this is a letter that belongs in the New Testament canon, and its thoughts, advice and examples have great authority. So what does the writer of the letter, writing in the name of Paul, have to say about Alexander the coppersmith?

'Alexander the coppersmith did me great harm; the Lord will pay him back for his deeds. You also must beware of him, for he strongly opposed our message.' The implication is that the writer is now very wary of Alexander and is urging Timothy and his companions to do the same. The bit about the Lord paying him back for his deeds is perhaps a shade less than perfect religion: it seems to imply, 'I will not pay him back, but I confidently leave it to the Lord to do so for me!'

The main point of interest and help in this little episode is in the word 'beware'. Jesus bids us to love our enemies, and yet here is an authentic interpreter of Jesus saying to beware of an enemy. We are not expected to suddenly become best friends with someone who has done us great harm. Pray for him, certainly. Be civil to him, perhaps – although Jesus was hardly civil to the scribes, Pharisees and Sadducees. Fully expect and hope to share heaven with him where forgiveness is all. But Jesus does not expect us to be able to write off great harms as if nothing has happened.

I think this 'beware' is a consoling word to hang on to. If someone has done us great harm, trying to make peace can lead to the other person just doing the same again. Someone calls me a cruel name; I make it clear how badly I was hurt; the bully may well call me the same name again, or worse. No point asking for trouble.

Family feuds can be very bitter, about almost nothing to begin with, very often. A truce of 'beware' can be more positive than perpetual sorrow over the strained relationship. Pray for the other side, have kind and respectful feelings about them, but don't feel in any hurry to get back to a normal family relationship. That is what this New Testament letter seems to me to be advising.

Another feature of this letter to Timothy is that Paul does not expect Alexander the coppersmith to apologise or to say he is sorry for what he did. We can break our hearts saying, 'If only the one who hurt me would apologise and say sorry.' But for Jesus, forgiveness comes first; saying sorry may or may not follow. He forgave his murderers when they had no notion of saying they were sorry.

TWENTY-FIVE

The star comes and goes

Matthew 2:1-12

I suppose many of us first hear as children this story of the wise men who come from the East to bring gifts to the infant king in Bethlehem. As children, our imaginations are fresh and colourful. We can picture the wise men (are there only three?) as star-gazers fond of studying late at night when the stars would be at their brightest. They would have their star-maps, devised by previous astrologers, to show which star belongs where, and also to show if any star turns up in a part of the sky where it is not expected.

As children, we would not be troubled by what exactly was the nature of the new light in the heavens that they saw, as the story goes. Even we knew that most of the stars winked at us, but the ones called planets did not wink: instead they had a way of wandering from one cluster of stars to another, in a regular pattern. So why should not the wise men, the Magi, when they see a new brilliant star, wonder what it means? Perhaps they connect the star, as Matthew the storyteller does, with the one that was prophesied by the prophet Balaam when his donkey would not budge (Numbers 22:23-7): a star that would tell of a new ruler one day in the Holy Land.

So the wise men (are they all men?) set out to see for themselves, taking gifts of gold, frankincense and myrrh. They set out by night and travel by night, as they want to be sure of following the star. Who knows how many camels they have, how many servants? No doubt they take good note of the route they are following, because they intend to come home the same way after they have paid homage and presented their gifts.

Then they seem to lose track of their star. They are near to Jerusalem, which is where they would expect to find the newborn king. So they make enquiries, and are advised to go to Bethlehem. On the way there they see the star again, and are full of joy: it points them to exactly where they should go.

Even as children we can find a comforting message in the story: when we are happy and consoled, we can follow our star; when it disappears, we need patience and good hope – maybe we need to ask someone who might know the answer, what happened to my star? But if we trust and pray, the star always comes back and leads us in joy to where Jesus is.

Ignatius of Loyola in his first rules for discernment of spirits (in his *Spiritual Exercises*) advises us not to be careless when we are happy and consoled by the gift of God. Best to remember that consolation comes and goes, so store up the memories of how good it feels, and of how sure you are that all will be well in the end. Consolation will come back, so be patient when it seems to disappear.

The image of the star – clear, then missing, then shining brightly again – is a helpful one to remember when we seem to lose our way.

TWENTY-SIX

Wine and water

John 2:1-11

According to today's reading, Jesus at the wedding feast in Cana changed water into wine. He was a guest at the wedding, and his mother, also a guest, was embarrassed for the wedding couple and the groom's family, because the wine had run out before the feast was ended. She asked Jesus to do something about the situation so as to keep the day as a happy day, unmarred by a sudden cessation of joy.

So, according to the story, Jesus changed a large quantity of water, of which there was plenty, into a large quantity of wine. The account emphasises that the quality of Jesus' wine was every bit as good as the wine the family had provided, and indeed better. This made Jesus' disciples, who were there with him, believe in him: this was the first of the signs that revealed his glory.

So what is the significance of what Jesus does that day? What does it all mean – water, wine, wedding? Take the wedding first: the story does seem to indicate that Jesus is on the side of joy rather than being a killjoy. He may be reluctant to show his hand before the time he has planned, but he allows himself to be persuaded by his mother nonetheless.

And what about the water and the wine? If this is a sign, what is the significance? Surely, Jesus is demonstrating that he is here to upgrade what he finds to something more costly, more precious. We have only to think – supposing at the start of the meal Jesus turns all the wine into water, instead of the other way round, then everybody would have felt cheated. Jesus has come to transform watery human nature into sharing the divine life of God: water into wine, not the other way round.

Catholic churches have from earliest days presented water as well as wine in preparing the gifts for the Eucharist. You can't get much earlier than Justin Martyr or Irenaeus, who both travelled to churches in different countries, and who both said the one presiding takes a cup of wine mixed with water – that is what is always done. So at the start of the Eucharist you have bread ready for 'This is my body', water for Jesus' human life, and wine to become his divine life. Then the opening prayer asks that as Jesus when he was born took on our 'water', so may we come to share in his 'wine'. He became human for us so that we could become sharers in his divinity.

I have for years campaigned against the way the offertory prayer over the wine speaks about it as 'made by human hands'. I would be happy to wager that there is no Christian or Jewish prayer before 1970 that says that wine is 'made by hands'. The early Christian writers said that wine is 'engendered by God' or 'heavenly'. Jesus implies the same by upgrading earthly water to divine wine. Otherwise the offertory prayers are making the exchange between one thing made by hands and another thing made by hands – so that there is only progress from human life to more human life. There is more to wine than grape juice.

TWENTY-SEVEN

The narrow gate

Matthew 7:13, 14

These sayings of Jesus about the narrow gate appear in the Sermon on the Mount – notably, 'the gate is narrow and the road is hard that leads to life, and there are few who find it.' He tells us to enter through the narrow gate, even though many take the option of the easy road that leads to destruction.

Surely Jesus is not recommending his disciples to strain every nerve to enter into life, to enter into the kingdom, then having arrived there to rejoice in their own safety and at having left the majority of the human race behind? Disciples of Jesus are meant to be helping the cause of Jesus.

We can presume that Jesus' own progress through life involved going through the narrow gate, but Jesus was bent on saving the whole world. We cannot think of him suffering, dying and rising again, then ascending to God's right hand just to sit back and say, 'I made it; a pity about the rest of humankind!'

The idea of the narrow gate must be connected to the missionary and apostolic side of the kingdom: go by the hard road and enter by the narrow gate in order to find safety for yourself, but also to make it possible for those who have not tried, to be forgiven through relying on the mercy of God.

There are many mothers who are faithful to their Christian life through thick and thin, who hope and pray for their sons and daughters even though the children have taken the easy road and seem to be headed for destruction. For such mothers, as for Jesus, there would be small consolation being finally in heaven without the sons and daughters they love. Saint Monica, mother of Saint Augustine, was fortunate enough to see her son switch to the narrow gate, but very many mothers just have to live and die in hope.

The key story of the prodigal son shows Jesus expecting the elder brother, who had taken the hard road, to join the celebrations for his younger brother who had taken the easy road (Luke 15:11-32). Any hard-working Christian may look forward to a heaven shared with people who do not deserve heaven. Really, of course, none of us deserves such a gift.

Anyone taking on a religious life or a vocation to the priesthood expects to work harder than average so as to carry along those who are only able to work less than the average. Something like this must be behind Jesus' instruction to carry another's burden an extra mile (Matthew 5:38-42): a Roman soldier orders me to carry his gear from one milestone to the next, as the Law allows. Then to his surprise I volunteer another mile, and what was a burden suddenly turns into an act of brotherly love.

TWENTY-EIGHT

Change and become like children

Matthew 18:3

Just about everyone who hears these words of Jesus has a different way of understanding them. 'Truly I tell you, unless you change and become like children, you will never enter the kingdom of heaven.' For me the key to understanding the words is to be found in the two versions of the Lord's Prayer. In Matthew's version (Matthew 6:9-13), we say together, 'Our Father', speaking as a church, speaking as a body. In Luke's version (Luke 11:2-4), each of us on our own is saying, 'Father', 'my Father', in imitation of Jesus in the Garden of Gethsemane: '*Abba*!' (Mark 14:36). *Abba* was and still is in Israel the way a child would address the father of the family. The word implies trust and love. It states where I come from, and it takes for granted that I am as much loved as any of my brothers and sisters.

Nobody in the history of the world before Jesus ever dared to call God by such a familiar name, yet here is Jesus saying that unless we do so we will never enter the kingdom of heaven. The traditional introduction to the Lord's Prayer at the Eucharist states that we are daring when we call God 'Our Father'. How much more daring it is when we call God *Abba*, but we can do it because Jesus told us to. This, surely, is the change in ourselves that we have to make in order to enter the kingdom of heaven.

The relationship of child/*Abba* reaches through passage after passage of the Gospels. Thus when three men are given talents and one of them does not trust the donor, the untrusting one ends up in serious trouble (Matthew 25:14-30). If he were to look upon the donor as *Abba*, he would trade with his talent without fear. Jesus speaks rough judgements on some of the towns that do not listen to him (Matthew 10:11-15) because they too are unwilling to think of God as *Abba*. The five foolish bridesmaids call upon the king as so many servants who are late for the wedding (Matthew 25:11), when they should plead as beloved daughters, and be let in.

Another thing about children that Jesus would have in mind is their willingness to be held by the hand and led. For a child, life is usually more exciting when it is an adult-led expedition. Jesus teaches a Way –

in fact, he teaches The Way – and unless he leads us by the hand along it we cannot hope to show it afterwards to anyone else. If we change and become like children, saying after saying of Jesus opens up its meaning to us.

Jesus makes clear that it is not enough, when we are being judged, to plead 'Lord! Lord . . . I did this for you; I did that for you!' (see Matthew 7:21-3) when all along the Holy Spirit our Advocate is urging us to cry out '*Abba*! Father!' and to rely instead on the priceless relationship with God that is freely offered to us by Jesus.

TWENTY-NINE

'Feed my lambs'

John 21:15

Lambs, sheep, under-shepherds and shepherds feature a lot in the Bible, not least in the sayings about Jesus. Already in the Old Testament the people of Israel are spoken of as being the sheep of God's pasture. God is distressed if the appointed shepherds neglect the sheep, choosing to look after themselves at the expense of the sheep. There follows a promise that either God will come in person to shepherd the sheep in future, or else God's son David will rise again and take charge of the flock.

When Jesus 'son of David' comes to take charge, he sees a crowd of thousands in front of him, and he has pity on them because they are 'like sheep without a shepherd' (Mark 6:34). He is the shepherd; the thousands are the sheep. He makes them lie down on the green grass, and there, where there is plenty of water, he feeds them on plentiful bread with fish for flavouring. Immediately around him are his 12 chosen apostles, and they are given a share in the work of feeding the 'lambs' and the 'sheep'. So we have Jesus as the shepherd and his apostles as under-shepherds, or perhaps as we in western countries might say, he the shepherd and his apostles his sheepdogs.

The work of feeding and tending the lambs and the sheep in Jesus' community is not confined to the apostles. Every new Christian is baptised into the flock as one who will be cared for and fed, but sooner or later the invitation or the inspiration comes to care for others in the kindly way they themselves were cared for. In other words, a new Christian counts as a lamb or a sheep and eventually is called upon to become a shepherd. The strange fact is that the sheep becomes a shepherd without ceasing to be a lamb or a sheep.

Lambs do not become shepherds by a natural progression. A lamb grows into a sheep, not into a shepherd. We are talking about a second gift, over and above nature, over and above the first gift. The first gift is to be a lamb under the watchful, loving eye of the shepherd. The second gift is for the lamb to become a shepherd, able to give to others the loving care it received earlier.

A shepherd who loves his sheepdog is usually indulgent to a dog who makes a mistake. They will remain friends and there will be opportunities to make amends. We could compare on the human level the way Jesus in the resurrection gives his under-shepherd Peter a fresh start. Peter went 'back to square one', and is asked all over again to feed Jesus' lambs.

It does seem that if I make a poor job of feeding or tending the flock, I can fall back on the ever-present fact of the first gift, namely that the shepherd will come looking for me, to bring me back – his lost sheep.

THIRTY

Shine a light

Matthew 5:14-16

There are often two sides to the Gospel images chosen by Jesus. From one point of view, we are all sheep belonging to Jesus' sheepfold; from another point of view we are called to be shepherds, willing and able to look after the welfare of others. There are many other images with two sides to them, and one of these is the image of light.

The light shines on each one of us when we are baptised; then Jesus invites us to shine the light on everyone else in the house. We are even given a candle of our very own as part of the ceremony of baptism. Babies being baptised do not hold their candle, but one day they will understand that the light of the candle stands for enlightenment of the mind: from now on I may know myself as God's child – God's son or God's daughter, with my own place at God's family table, which can never be removed. An early Christian name for baptism was 'enlightenment': you were enlightened as to who you really were.

To have the water of baptism and then the candlelight is very comforting. To hold the candle close to my breast means also that the warmth of the candle can be felt. To be chosen as God's own child is heart-warming, and it is meant to be so.

But then comes the other side of Jesus' image of light. In the Sermon on the Mount he asks us not to be like someone hiding their light under a basket or a bucket but to put it on a lampstand or to hold it up, so it will shine for everyone else in the house.

Obviously, giving everyone else the benefit of my candlelight is not as comforting as it is to have the light all to myself. I must try to enlighten everyone around me, that they too can be children of God. The second side of Jesus' images is always more difficult than the first. Being a shepherd is more difficult than being a sheep; shining a light is more difficult than basking in the light.

Another way of looking at being light for others is to imagine myself as a mirror. All that God wants me to know has been told to me; I know it applies not just to me but to any other person alive, so I set about reflecting God's message to me so that it shines on other receptive people. After a time, maybe only after years of passing on the loving message, the mirror can begin to feel cold, but the faithful message still shines through. One thing the 'mirror' image makes clear is that if the message is not coming through, the mirror can only go back to the source for strength: the mirror cannot create God's message; it can only reflect it.

THIRTY-ONE

Bread, then wine

Luke 22:19, 20

For many centuries, the faithful lay people of the Catholic Church received communion under one kind alone, namely under the form of bread. The communion wine was restricted to the priest presiding at the Eucharist. At the time of the Reformation, the reformers restored the chalice to the people, but the Roman Catholic authorities refused to go along with this. For another five centuries or so the Catholic faithful received communion only in the form of bread.

It was not until 1970, after the Second Vatican Council, that the privilege taken by the reformers was extended to ordinary Catholics who wished to receive from the chalice. When that happened, many Catholics chose not to drink from the chalice when it was offered to them. They had been taught as children that Jesus was received whole and entire 'under either kind alone'. From this they concluded that nothing was to be gained from taking the wine as well as the bread. The wine was a novelty, the cup a dubious health hazard, and the whole thing was something done in the Reformed churches, and therefore suspect.

Catholics have grown more used to taking the chalice as the decades have gone by. There is no escaping the fact that Jesus wanted all his disciples to celebrate his new covenant with both bread and wine, not bread alone. There are many reasons why bread and wine fit together and complement one another, and one of the most beautiful goes like this:

Jesus received as bread is a sign of Jesus dead. Yes, Jesus alive is there, but the bread signifies his body without the blood, according to Jesus' own words. Without the blood means Jesus on the cross, Jesus taken down from the cross, Jesus in the tomb, Jesus who died for us. In receiving Jesus in the form of bread I am welcoming Jesus who died for me, Jesus who loved me first, Jesus who made no conditions and who continues to make no conditions to his love.

The normal order of things is that the communicant then goes to where a priest, a deacon or another appointed minister is proffering the chalice. Here the signs have a different meaning. 'Can you drink the cup that I drink?' is what Jesus is saying now. One of the psalms expresses the situation beautifully: 'What shall I return to the Lord for all his bounty to me? I will lift up the cup of salvation and call on the name of the Lord' (Psalm 116:12-13). Taking the chalice means the communicant is deeply grateful for the love shown on the cross by Jesus, and wishes to repay Jesus by living in his way.

Why wine? Wine is intoxicating, and in 'sign' terms this indicates that Yes, we wish to live as perfect Christians but we do not have the inner strength to love Jesus as he first loved us. We need to be intoxicated: 'Blood of Christ, intoxicate me' as the old prayer *Anima Christi* puts it. The Spirit that Jesus sends will enable us to do the impossible.

THIRTY-TWO

'The truth will make you free'

John 8:32

Christian baptism celebrates the fact that we are God's children and that from now on we may enjoy the freedom of the children of God. We do not have to earn the right to be called God's children; indeed, we could never earn such a privilege, no matter how hard we tried. Jesus used many images to talk about baptism, and all of them come to us freely.

We are God's lambs, and we are to be fed; we do not have to earn the milk or the grass in the green pastures. We are enlightened, learning truths that are beyond our human minds to imagine, so we could not learn them by ourselves. We are told to be like little children, and Jesus was delighted that his Father chose such to receive his revelation. We are revealed as first-generation daughters and sons of God, and that comes to us as a free gift or not at all. There is no way we could earn such an infinite gift.

As children believing we are God's children we are built on a rock. God's love for his children is the most rock-like reality in existence. And yet, though rocks are among the most permanent things on Earth, even they can crumble in an earthquake. Not so God's love, which is everlasting.

Another image Jesus used was that of fishing: the apostles Peter and Andrew, James and John would go from catching fish to catching people (Matthew 4:21). The four of them were 'caught in his net' by Jesus, like little fish.[5] They did not know yet what Jesus was offering: he chose them; they did not choose him.

We are like an empty field, or perhaps a weed-filled field, and unless Jesus the sower fills us with good seed, we remain unfruitful.

Jesus is the Way, and he instructs us as to how to find the Way for ourselves. Without him we would never find it on our own.

All these are images of the free gift of God. How do they make us free? Well, when it comes to responding to such a gift, we may picture the task in the same metaphors as above: we are lambs called to be shepherds; we are enlightened and called to pass on the enlightenment;

---

5. G. O'Mahony, *The Two Edged Gospel: Gift and Invitation* (Gracewing: Leominster, 2005).

we are little children called to exercise delegated power; we are sons and daughters invited to act as servants; standing on rock we can be rock-like for others; we are on the watch with our nets to catch other 'fish' for Jesus when they swim past us; we work and pray that our empty field will yield a good harvest; having noted and experienced the Way of Jesus we are willing and happy to show it to others.

And free? We are children of the king; we are not slaves. If our response to God's love as we look back has not been very good, then we are free not to run away in shame but to keep on trying, trusting in the way a little child would trust its parents. After all, the gift is free, but the response is costly, and often beyond our own powers. We need power, a second gift, from the Holy Spirit sent by Jesus.

THIRTY-THREE

The house built on rock

Matthew 7:24-7

Everyone who hears the words of Jesus and acts on them will be like a man who built his house on rock. Nature can throw what it will against the house: floods, storms, wild winds can come, and the house will stay firm on its foundations.

Suppose we unwrap Jesus' parable and ask ourselves which are the words of Jesus he wants us to hear as we build our house, and also how we are to act on them. This has to do with confidence and hope. What are the sayings of Jesus that help us to stand up and look the world in the eye, and not go to pieces when illness comes, or poverty, or the failure of human plans?

His Father is our Father: that has to be where our foundation lies. Jesus himself is our brother, and we are all his brothers and sisters. What anybody does to the least of us, if it is good, he will thank them. However we might be left behind by the rest of the world, Jesus will be with me the least one, and will stay behind with me the lost one. These are fundamental promises from Jesus, and we can rely on them.

When it comes to promises made by Jesus' apostles and other early disciples, there is a wealth of images to do with permanence. We were chosen in Christ before the foundation of the world (Ephesians 1:4). We are God's work of art, and part of his household (Ephesians 2:10). We are told time and again not to be afraid. Jesus is the fulfilment of God's promise; he is the Redeemer, so swollen rivers and raging fire cannot touch us (Isaiah 43:1-4). God his Father has loved us with an everlasting love, the kind of love good parents have for their children, and even if a human father or mother should ever turn against a child of theirs, still God's love will be settled and unchanging (Psalm 27:10).

Jesus expects us to pass on to the rest of the world the same rock-like love that has been shown to us. He implies that if my feet are standing on rock, not on shifting sand, then I am in a position to lead others to stand where I stand – in a relationship with God that is trusting. There are, of course, hundreds of sayings of Jesus telling us how to relate to one another. Probably the most important is to know myself forgiven, and therefore to pass on to others that priceless gift. I need it in any case, because there are so many instructions of Jesus that I do not keep well enough myself. I will never persuade an enquirer to come and follow Jesus if they think they have to be perfect in every detail, but a forgiven sinner – forgiven every time – is on a very firm foundation.

We are invited by Mark's Gospel, and also by Paul writing to the Romans and the Galatians, to call God *Abba* as Jesus did – the intimate name a little child would call its well-loved father (Mark 13:35; Romans 8:15; Galatians 4:6). Jesus' Sermon on the Mount alone has about 37 instructions as to how to live his life (Matthew 5–7). The only way we can promise to obey so many rules is to rely on God's forgiveness each time we fail. The only way we can be a rock for others is to pass on to them the same forgiveness that is shown by God to us.

THIRTY-FOUR

Who is right?

Luke 18:9-14

When we read the Gospels, it becomes clear that there is more to pleasing God than just the exact fulfilling of the commandments and rules of religion. Take the story of the prodigal son, for instance (Luke 15:11-32). As Jesus tells the story, the younger brother broke every rule in the book: asking for his inheritance before his father died and then squandering his fortune on a wasteful life. The elder brother has been working away in the family field for years with no help at all from the younger brother. Yet when the young one comes back in distress, the father throws a party and a feast for him. The implication is that the young man is back in the family now, and his misdeeds forgiven. In the story, the father stands for the attitude Jesus the storyteller approves of. Jesus wants sinners to be forgiven and rejoiced over, even more than he approves of all the hard work the elder brother has done.

Put it this way: if we arrive at the gates of heaven after a lifetime of trying to be good, we are likely to find heaven well populated with forgiven sinners who apparently never tried to live a good life. And we will have to rejoice at finding them there, because there will be nowhere else for us to go.

The parable Jesus told about the labourers in the vineyard (Matthew 20:1-16) contains the same caution for those who think they are the only ones to be counted because they have worked the hardest. They worked all day in the heat and were promised a denarius each – a just day's wage for an unskilled worker. But then, because those who were hired at the eleventh hour received the same wage, the all-day crew were not a bit pleased. In this tale, Jesus' stance is with the landowner: his message is that heaven and a life with God is a generous gift, which nobody can earn by trying. It is not up to us mortals to decide who belongs and who does not: we are to take what we are given and stop comparing gifts as if they were rewards, and as if we are the ones to judge who is more deserving.

Yet another parable told by Jesus tells the same story, namely the one about the two men who went up to the temple to pray: the Pharisee and the tax-collector. The Pharisee was thankful that he was not villainous like the rest of the world, and in particular that he was not like the tax collector. He, the Pharisee, paid his tithes and he fasted twice a week. He stood at the front of the temple and told God how good he was. The tax collector, however, stood far off and did not even raise his eyes to heaven. He beat his breast and prayed, 'God, be merciful to me, a sinner!' Jesus judged that the tax collector was the one who went away justified.

As in the other two stories, Jesus sees something more important than correctness. The good news of Jesus is good news for sinners, but less than good news for the self-righteous unless they learn to share in Jesus' mission to save sinners.

THIRTY-FIVE

Peter the Rock

John 1:42

When Jesus gave his follower Simon son of John a new name – Peter, meaning Rock – the new name did not seem very appropriate. The Gospel stories that follow show Peter as spontaneous and sometimes tactless, thinking he could speak for all, even though he often missed the point that Jesus was making.

Peter could be sublime on occasion, as when he was inspired to see Jesus as 'You are the Messiah, the Son of the living God' (Matthew 16:16). But then, moments later, he stood in the way of Jesus, Messiah or not, saying that Jesus should not go anywhere near Jerusalem. It was a case of the disciple confidently trying to put his master right.

Peter was always chosen as a witness, as for the raising of Jairus' daughter (Mark 5:37), or the Transfiguration of Jesus (Matthew 17:1-7), or the agony of Jesus in the Garden of Gethsemane (Mark 14:32-3). He averred that even if the rest of the 12 were to desert Jesus, he would never do such a thing (Mark 14:29). Earlier on he had problems with Jesus' teachings on riches (Mark 10:24), and on how many times in the day Jesus expected him to forgive anyone who offended him (Matthew 18:21-2).

Along with the others, Peter was not happy at the thought of the brothers James and John wanting preferential treatment (Mark 10:35-41).

When Jesus was arrested and taken to the palace of the high priest, Peter followed along. Here is what he later said about himself: I was sitting with the guards and warming myself at the fire. One of the maids of the high priest came; seeing me warming myself she looked at me and said, 'You also were with the Nazarene, Jesus.' But I denied it, saying, 'I neither know nor understand what you mean.' And I went out into the gateway. And the maid saw me and began to say to the bystanders, 'This man is one of them.' But again I denied it. And after a little while again the bystanders said to me, 'Certainly you are one of them; for you are a Galilean.' But I began to invoke a curse on myself and to swear, 'I do not know this man of whom you speak.' And immediately the cock crowed a second time. And I remembered how

Jesus had said to me, 'Before the cock crows twice, you will deny me three times.' And I broke down and wept (Mark 14:66-72).[6]

We know that Jesus forgave Peter there on the spot, and again surely during the appearance of Jesus risen on Easter Sunday ('The Lord has risen indeed, and has appeared to Simon' – Luke 24:34) and later, explicitly, by the lake of Galilee when he treated Peter and the other six fishermen to breakfast (John 21:4-17).

That must have been the moment when Peter truly became a Rock. He had great love and affection for Jesus, he had been treating himself as the leader and spokesman for the 12, and in denying Jesus he had done the very worst thing he could ever imagine. Yet Jesus had forgiven him, with no recriminations. There was nothing worse that Peter could imagine himself doing, so that meant nothing under the sun could separate him from the love, affection and forgiveness of Jesus. Peter no longer needed to fear his own weakness.

---

6. It is thought that Peter was the main source of information for the writer of Mark's Gospel. See G. O'Mahony, *Praying St Mark's Gospel*, first published by Geoffrey Chapman, imprint of Cassell, London and Christian Classics, Westminster, Maryland, 1990. Reprinted by Gujarat Sahitya Prakash, India, 1995.

THIRTY-SIX

The boy cured of epilepsy

Mark 9:14-29

Jesus comes down from the mountain of the transfiguration with Peter, James and John to find that the rest of the disciples are in trouble. They are unable to cure a boy who has been brought to them suffering from epilepsy. According to the father of the boy, he has been afflicted not from birth but from childhood. Since then, from time to time a spirit comes over him and makes him unable to speak; it dashes him to the ground and makes him foam and grind his teeth and become rigid. The father of the boy relates all this to Jesus, now that Jesus has joined the crowd.

Jesus asks for the boy to be brought to him, and as soon as he comes near Jesus the boy is thrown into convulsions: he falls to the ground and rolls about, foaming at the mouth. The father continues to list the symptoms of the malady: 'It has often cast him into the fire, and into the water, to destroy him; but if you can do anything, have pity on us and help us.' Jesus says he can help anyone who has faith. Whereupon the father makes the prayer that has become so famous: 'I believe; help my unbelief!'

Then Jesus commands the spirit to come out of the boy, the spirit that prevents him from hearing and from speaking. The boy falls to the ground in terrible convulsions and ends up looking like a corpse. Then Jesus raises him up and gives him back to his father.

Epilepsy often starts in childhood. Fire is dangerous because under an attack the sufferers cannot feel the flames; nor can they be aware that they are drowning when in water. In an epileptic attack they cannot hear, nor can they speak; they can only howl nonsense. 'Attack' is a better word than 'fit', because what happens to them feels more like an invasion than anything natural.

It is my own belief that this story, as told in Mark's Gospel, is a true story specially selected for inclusion by Peter himself. Peter becomes famously deaf and dumb in the high priest's courtyard when challenged by the high priest's maid and the bystanders (Mark 14:66-72). He is, unwisely, warming himself at the fire at the time. (Matthew's Gospel is the one that tells of Peter nearly drowning – Matthew 14:28-31). Peter at the fire does not foam at the mouth, but he does curse and swear an oath that he does not know Jesus.

Jesus tells the disciples that this kind of spirit can only be cast out by prayer. The right prayer on this occasion is the prayer of the boy's father. Peter enters the courtyard of the high priest having failed to pray over three hours in the garden with Jesus. Without the prayer, Peter is unable to resist the 'dumb and deaf spirit'. He would better have prayed to God to increase the little faith he had.

THIRTY-SEVEN

Old and new

Mark 2:21, 22

Jesus uses an illustration from domestic life, true in itself but also a useful illustration for a message of his own. No one with any sense would take a piece of unshrunk cloth and sew it on to an old cloak, to serve as a patch for the old. If that was done, the patch would pull away from the cloak, the new from the old, and the tear in the cloak would be worse, not better.

Likewise with new and old wine, and new or old wineskins. No one with any sense who wants to store new wine would put the new wine in old, dry skins. What would happen then would be that the new wine would burst the old wineskins and the wine would be lost, as well as the old wineskins. What one normally does, says Jesus, is to put new wine into fresh skins.

These two illustrations are placed by Mark in the midst of Jesus' early arguments with the scribes of the Pharisees. I think it is not stretching the meaning of the stories too much to guess that Jesus already has in mind the new covenant he will introduce, as opposed to the old covenant or covenants of Jewish history. Already Jesus is working in accordance with his new covenant, even though he has not yet given it the name of 'covenant'. And it is very new.

The new thing that Jesus brings from God is unconditional love and forgiveness. 'Son, your sins are forgiven. Daughter, your sins are forgiven.' No 'ifs', no 'buts', no 'on condition that', or 'provided that'. To the woman caught in adultery he says, 'Neither do I condemn you' (John 8:11). He tells her not to sin again, but this is not a condition of his forgiveness. To the small tax collector Jesus simply invites himself to a meal at his house and waits till the expected response arrives, in the middle of the meal (Luke 19:5-8). Even for those who kill Jesus, Jesus makes excuses: 'Father, forgive them; for they do not know what they are doing' (Luke 23:34).

The old covenant between God and the people of Israel was usually put in a conditional form by the rulers or prophets of the time. If the people transgressed or went worshipping strange Gods, then the anger of the Lord would be kindled against them and they would perish quickly from the good land he had given them.

Jesus takes what looks to us like a gamble. Forgive first, then repentance will follow. We always want repentance to be shown before we will forgive. Jesus is not taking a gamble because his way is the way God goes about forgiving. Even in Old Testament times, the prophets were always instructed to give the people another chance. They would not have been surprised at the coming of Jesus.

Jesus' new wine is too strong for those who are fixed in the old ways. Those who are happy to be forgiven for free are, so to speak, the new skins.

THIRTY-EIGHT

John beheaded

Mark 6:14-29

One thought that surely comes to anyone reading through Mark's Gospel is this: what is a barbaric story such as the beheading of John the Baptist doing in the good news? Yes, it is important, but we could have been spared the details.

But then, this story is written in the same chapter as the story of Jesus feeding the 5000. It seems to me that Mark puts the two stories side by side to highlight the differences between the two kings – Jesus and Herod – and between their two kingdoms.

Herod is a king in a part of the world where the king is thought of as shepherd of his people. Herod's motives are selfish. Jesus has compassion on the 5000 who have followed him because they are 'like sheep without a shepherd' (Mark 6:34). He is the shepherd-king whose first thought is for his subjects.

Herod and Jesus both hold a banquet. Invited to Herod's banquet are his courtiers, some army officers and leading persons in his kingdom – invitees only (verse 21). It takes place in his palace. Jesus invites to his banquet anyone at all who wishes to come – rich or poor, important or simple, healthy or sick. He makes them lie down on the green grass near the fresh water, like God in the twenty-third psalm, and first he teaches them.

Herod would certainly provide rich foods for his guests; it would be an expensive menu to show his wealth. Jesus provides bread, fish and water, but the food is free – it does not cost his guests anything at all. There is plenty over, which means that everyone in the crowd has enough to eat.

Jesus gives his listeners good news before he feeds them. His whole message is one of goodness, generosity and acceptance. The message from Herod's banquet, by contrast, is a message of lust, hatred, deafness to the words of a prophet, murder, and a severed head brought in on a plate. 'What a dainty dish to set before a king!'

Herod is a quisling king. He is not in the direct line of David but has been appointed by the Roman conquerors. Jesus is the Son of David, promised and authorised by the prophets and their predictions about the King, the Shepherd who was to come.

So it seems to me that Mark goes into such detail regarding the way John the Baptist died, not just to share with us the information he has about the death of a martyr, but to point out and underline how the kingship of Jesus differs radically from the style of an earthly king. We are left asking ourselves, to which of the two kings would I rather give my allegiance?

THIRTY-NINE

Many inns

John 14:2

Dorothy L. Sayers was a writer of detective novels that featured Lord Peter Wimsey as her clever detective. She also wrote a beautiful play for radio, entitled *The Man Born to be King*, which brought Jesus and his disciples to life using the words of the Gospels and filling them out to make them sound like everyday speech. I was only a child when I first heard the play, but one sentence has stayed in my memory: 'On the way to my Father's house there are many inns, and I go ahead to prepare a place for you.'

Dorothy Sayers was also a scholar of classical languages and times, so she felt she was not out of line translating *pollai monai* not as 'many mansions' or as 'many dwelling places', but as 'many inns'. The original Greek can mean many places where you remain, or many places where you stop for a while. To think of Jesus meaning 'many inns' opens up a whole new picture. This is not now about heavenly mansions at the very end of our journey, but about a continuous journey prepared for us by Jesus, who has gone ahead and booked us in to each and every inn along the way.

The most dramatic of the inns in the Gospels is the one on the road from Jerusalem to Jericho. Whenever we find ourselves feeling as if we have been mugged, fallen among thieves and left to bleed to death, along comes a 'good Samaritan' by the Providence of God (Luke 10:29-37). There is the kind of inn to which we may be brought to recuperate.

But there are many inns in our lives that are not so dramatic. These are simply the holidays, the breaks, the days off – those times when, even though we are not working, we are conscious of Jesus' approval. Even some days out can have the feeling of being booked ahead by Jesus.

The disciples listening to Jesus at the Last Supper discourse are wondering about where they are to go, where indeed they are going. What Jesus gives them is a way of life based on his own life. If they follow him, they will find clues all along the way to reassure them that they are in the right place, at the right time, doing the right thing. There will be a sense at every inn or stopping place that Jesus has been there not long ago and booked them in as guests – that he has been expecting them to turn up in that very place at around that very time.

Jesus seems to lead from the front, not just like a gallant army general but more like an adult, a big brother, moving ahead but constantly encouraging a little brother or sister to follow. He turns to face the little one and says, 'Come on; it's all right. I've been here before you and it's all right. The next inn is just round the corner.'

'Do not let your hearts be troubled', because there is always another inn, and there is always the presence of Jesus, until the day when we finally catch up with Jesus and can live where he lives, with no more packing up and moving on.

FORTY

Jesus good Samaritan

Luke 10:29-37

We have just heard Jesus tell the story of the good Samaritan. Our first reaction is to feel drawn by Jesus to 'Go and do likewise.' We have seen the courage and humanity of this foreigner who rescued the fallen Jew with as much tenderness and generosity as if he had been another Samaritan. We are being called to help anyone we find to be in deep trouble, without asking where they come from or whether they are friend or foe.

There is another way of thinking about the parable, which comes to the same conclusion in the end but which provides an even greater incentive to be compassionate: that is to contemplate how like Jesus himself is the good Samaritan in his story. Jesus, good Samaritan, comes to the rescue of me, of us, of the human race in our fallen state.

Jesus came as foreigner into our world, in a manner of speaking. His nature is divine; he comes from a world where love and forgiveness rule, into our world where goodness and malice exist side by side. He comes across a man who has fallen foul of robbers, who lies stripped and beaten and has been left to die. Jesus does not say, 'This has nothing to do with me: this man is of a different race from me.' Jesus sets about rescuing him – rescuing me – the fallen one, with bandages, with wine and with oil. The whole of Jesus' life is dedicated to raising the fallen human race, whom he recognises as his brothers and sisters. It is comforting to recall the times and places in my life when Jesus has rescued me from distressing circumstances and bound up my wounds.

Picture, then, how Jesus lifts me or you onto his own animal and carefully leads the horse or mule to the inn along the way to Jericho. After traumatic events in our lives we need a place of respite, somewhere to recover. Perhaps you, like me, can recall quiet places where you have been able to recover from rough treatment. In the story, Jesus enlists the innkeeper (and probably the innkeeper's wife) to see me, or you, safely to a night's rest, and our good Samaritan stays on watch till morning.

In the morning the Samaritan produces money for the innkeeper, enough for himself and for the wounded one. In a way this is what Jesus also does, leaving me, leaving us, with no debt to be paid to God.

What is more, he says to the innkeeper that he will be coming that way again, and if any further debt is incurred, he will settle it then. This to me seems to say that Jesus also is coming back this way: not bringing a threat but bringing release from any debts incurred between now and then.

What it comes to is this: the good Samaritan is not just a parable made up by Jesus; it is based on what Jesus himself did, what he does, what he will do. So when I am invited to go and do likewise, I am invited to imitate not just a story but Jesus himself, the storyteller who risked his very life for me.

FORTY-ONE

Ten bridesmaids

Matthew 25:1-13

A Jewish family I once knew had particular thoughts about some of Jesus' sayings. For instance, when they heard the story about the ten bridesmaids, five of them wise and five foolish, they immediately pictured Jesus holding up his two hands. 'Five of them were foolish,' (here he holds up his left hand and its five fingers) 'and five of them were wise' (here he holds up his right hand with its five fingers). I suppose most people have one hand that could be called 'wise' and the other one 'foolish'. For me, the right hand does what I ask it to quite skilfully, whereas my left hand tends to be clumsy or sleepy.

Hearing what my Jewish friends thought about the ten bridesmaids made me think again about what Jesus is saying: is it something quite different from the line I had always taken? Is Jesus not talking about half the human race entering into heaven, whereas the other half after a foolish life would be excluded from heaven? Is he not rather talking about each person alive being a mixture of wise and foolish, clever and stupid, skilful and clumsy? The story now becomes similar to another parable of Jesus in which the same field has good wheat and bad weeds (Matthew 13:24-30). That could not be meant to picture 'good people' and 'bad people', since that would mean many are damned from the start, since weeds do not become good wheat: there would be no room for repentance. We are all a combination of right hand and left hand.

In the story about the bridesmaids, the five excluded come to the door and cry, 'Lord, lord, open to us.' How can we bring them inside? Surely if my right hand is welcomed, my left hand cannot be shut out? I think the clue is in the word the bridesmaids use to call on the bridegroom, namely 'Lord'. They are admitting that they are servants, and that they have failed in their duties. If faithful service is the key to entry to the wedding, they have no key. Is there any alternative?

What about calling upon the Advocate that Jesus promised and then sent from heaven? The Advocate, the lawyer for the defence, the Holy Spirit. The one who enables us to call God '*Abba*! Father!' Our right hand claims heaven as a right, but our left hand reminds us that we are clueless servants. But if we put the two together and know God as our first-generation Father, and Jesus the Bridegroom as our very own brother, then we will not be shut out when we plead to come in to the wedding. The key to entry does not lie in whether we are good servants or not, but in our relationship with God, which is pure gift.

FORTY-TWO

Jesus became poor

2 Corinthians 8:9

Jesus was rich, but he became poor so that we poor people could become rich. According to the signs and images we use at the Eucharist, we say that Jesus was rich like wine, but he came to unite with our watery lives so that we could be united with his wine. As the Christmas carol puts it, 'He left all his glory behind, to be born and to die for mankind.'[7]

Poverty was not only for Jesus, but it was also recommended by Jesus for anyone who wants to be perfect. 'Go, sell what you own, and give the money to the poor, and you will have treasure in heaven; then come, follow me.' This was said by Jesus to the rich man who came inquiring, but the thought was too much for the man, and he went away sad (Mark 10:17-22).

The wish of Jesus was taken up and taken seriously by the early Church, the Church that came into being in Jerusalem after the resurrection and ascension of Jesus. 'All who believed were together and had all things in common; they would sell their possessions and goods and distribute the proceeds to all, as any had need' (Acts 2:44-5). The only trouble was, as a community they went bankrupt. Jesus himself had relied for his daily needs and those of his closest followers on a group of well-to-do women who provided for him out of their resources. The same need for backup is a reality today: anyone wishing to join a Christian religious community is relying on the generosity shown now or in the past by wealthier people providing a basic fund to enable the new member to have no money of his or her own. This is begging, but on a big scale. Paul in his second letter to the Corinthians is asking them to be generous in helping to bail out the Jerusalem community; however, he does not ask them to beggar themselves, only to give what they have over and above their own needs.

There is a second way of being poor, which is recommended for everybody by Jesus. We are all called to see ourselves as children of God, as brothers and sisters of Jesus. No one of us has more right than anyone else to the treasures of this world: the sun, the moon, the stars,

---

7. From the carol 'Come, come, come to the manger' (anonymous, 19th century).

water, a roof overhead, food, energy, security – all these and many more. Therefore we should be willing to take no more than our fair share of the gifts, and willing to let go of what is more than our fair share. That, I think, is the essence of what is called 'spiritual poverty'. This ideal must be behind Jesus' telling us to be willing to lend, and to be content not to ask for the return of goods we have loaned (Luke 6:35). It is also an ideal that still reproaches us for indulging in costly new toys while so many millions under the same sky go hungry.

There is a third kind of poverty, one that Jesus insists on: I call it poverty of merit. Being good is a gift from God; it is not something we human beings can guarantee. Jesus wants us not to pride ourselves on any good we have done, not to boast to God or to anyone else about our virtues. If we do boast, Jesus reckons we have had all the reward we will ever receive. Likewise, if we become sad or jealous of others because of our poor performance, we will lose heart and stop trying. The trick is to keep on trying to do good, and not to let our left hand know what our right hand has done.

FORTY-THREE

Recognising Jesus risen

John 20:16

There are slight discrepancies in the New Testament regarding the exact timing and placing of Jesus' appearances to his disciples after the resurrection. However, there is a kernel of evidence that all witnesses agree to. For instance, that Jesus was the Christ and that he died for our sins as the Scriptures had foretold; he was buried; he rose on the third day as the Scriptures said he would; he then appeared to the 11 apostles, with a special appearance or a special message to Peter; at least one of the appearances was to a large number of disciples; women were the first witnesses; the tomb was empty on the third day; and Jesus was difficult to recognise at first sight.

We need to muse about that last item: Jesus risen was difficult to recognise as being Jesus at first sight. Obviously the witnesses got past that problem, because all the apostles except John died a martyr's death rather than deny it was the same Jesus they saw when he rose from the dead. Pretty obviously, there was a block in the minds and imaginations of the witnesses, coming from the fact that they remembered or they knew Jesus had died a terrible death on the cross only days before. Human nature creates a closure on the memory of someone who is definitely dead. Jesus had said he would rise on the third day, but the disciples simply did not know what he meant until he actually rose.

Jesus risen seems to come and go regardless of times and places: his risen life is different in quality from his earlier way of being. He comes through closed doors. He brings an enormous and lasting sense of consolation to his friends, yet completely unexpectedly. They are not expecting this, and their hearts are broken until the moment when they each recognise him.

To me, the sweetest moment in the Gospels is the moment when Mary Magdalene recognises Jesus from the way he says her name – just, 'Mary'. The great painter Rembrandt pictures the moment – Jesus standing there in a floppy hat and big boots, holding a spade, so Mary can be forgiven for thinking he is the gardener. She has come to anoint his dead body now that the Sabbath is over, and she is distraught. But in that moment her life is changed and uplifted for ever.

There are several other recognition scenes in the Gospel accounts, such as Thomas verifying Jesus' wounds, the two disciples finally recognising Jesus after a walk to Emmaus with him, and the disciples who went fishing (John 20:26-9; Luke 24:13-35; John 21:4-8). To me, the wonderful thing about Jesus risen recognising his friends and being recognised by them is that Jesus promises us that his disciples will be with him where he is: he will come to take us there. And recognition will be part of it: we will not in dying be poured anonymously into the ocean of God's love; we will know him, and we will know one another.

FORTY-FOUR

Christ died for our sins

1 Corinthians 15:3-8

The apostle Paul tells us that in writing this letter to the converts of Corinth he is reminding them of things he learnt himself 15 years before – exactly as he had learnt them. Paul was converted to following the Way of Jesus just three years after Jesus' death and resurrection. He was then taught to repeat, as a kind of shorthand way of remembering the heart of the matter:

> that Christ died for our sins, in accordance with the scriptures, and that he was buried, and that he was raised on the third day in accordance with the scriptures, and that he appeared to Cephas, then to the twelve. Then he appeared to more than five hundred brothers and sisters at one time [many of whom were still around and able to verify]. Then he appeared to James, then to all the apostles. Last of all . . . he appeared also to me.

Paul calls this little catechism a deposit. This is what he had been taught 15 years earlier, and like a precious item deposited in a bank, the message had not altered at all in the meantime. There are other memories that other followers of the Way added, without at all changing the central message. For instance, the first people to see Jesus risen were the women who had followed Jesus in his ministry. Also, that the tomb where Jesus' dead body had been laid was open and empty on the Sunday morning, the third day. These, and all the memories from the four Gospels, are not tales that grew in the telling; they are carefully guarded central truths.

What does Paul mean, quoting what he was taught, when he says that 'Christ died for our sins'? For myself, I think of it this way: Jesus came from heaven not to condemn us but to save us, and particularly to forgive us. He believed in forgiving first, then asking for repentance and a new way of life. He did not work on the belief system of punishment leading to improvement. To those who could accept it, he was saying, 'Your sins are forgiven . . . now what are you going to do about that?!' 'Neither do I condemn you; but do not do it again.'

This is divine logic. We even have a saying in English: 'To err is human; to forgive, divine.' It was, and still is, a risky procedure in a world that is not greatly given to forgiveness. Jesus' enemies were people who had worked out how to stay in God's good books. They followed the rules to the letter, so they were all right; never mind about the millions who did not know the rules, nor the thousands who knew the rules but could not keep them. So to have Jesus saying that God forgives sinners before they have repented marked out Jesus as an enemy, to be eliminated before he infected the whole nation and the national religion.

This meant that either Jesus had to stop declaring sinners forgiven, or else he would be hounded to his death. Jesus died for giving a picture of God as everlastingly forgiving, and for refusing to alter his message. He came from God: he knew he was right. He rose again by a power only from God, and so God was agreeing with Jesus.

Our sins are forgiven. How, then, are we going to show our gratitude?

FORTY-FIVE

'I am generous'

Matthew 20:1-16

There is a very old prayer of the Church that counts on God's being generous. It comes in an ancient Eucharistic prayer which has been in regular use from as early as the fourth century of the Christian era. It is known today as the Roman Canon. The prayer within the prayer to God goes like this (my own translation from the Latin): 'And to us sinners, your servants, hoping as we do in the multitude of your mercies, please grant some share and company (in heaven) with your holy apostles and martyrs, and with all your saints. Please let us into their number, acting not as an estimator of merit but as a generous giver-out of pardon.'

The landowner in the parable of the labourers in the vineyard agreed with those who started work early in the morning that they would receive a fair wage for the day. In the evening he gave instructions to his manager that the same daily wage should be given to the others who had not worked the same hours, notably to those who had only been hired at the eleventh hour. The landowner was generous. Jesus said that this was the way things were done in the kingdom of heaven: we would not necessarily be paid by the hour, but rather according to the generosity of the one in charge.

The old prayer from the Roman Canon is most consoling, and very daring. It brings comfort to most of those who hear it spoken as an official prayer of the Church. As a Church we are asking God to let us into the kingdom, with all the holy apostles and saints and martyrs, not on the basis that we deserve to be let in, but simply because we rely on the generosity of God. The prayer asks God not to be an estimator of our merits, but to be a distributor (the Latin word is *largitor*, a giver of largesse) of forgiveness, and to admit us on that basis.

I said above that most people who hear the old prayer are comforted by hearing it, not least because this is an official prayer that has not been disputed or removed for centuries upon centuries. There is always a minority of hearers who either do not really listen to it, or else they ignore it if they do hear it. This was so in Jesus' story of the labourers: those who worked all day thought it was unfair that the latecomers should receive the same wage as themselves, who had 'borne the burden of the day and the scorching heat'.

More than once in the Gospel stories Jesus hopes that his followers will work hard, yes, but also that they will make room for others who, for one reason or another, are unable to do much in the way of meriting.

FORTY-SIX

God is . . . love is

1 Corinthians 13:4-9

Two and two make four, and there are two statements in the New Testament which, if you add them together, make an even richer message than the two on their own. 'God is love,' concludes John in his first letter (1 John 4:16), and 'Love is patient,' says Paul in this his first letter to the Corinthians. God is love, and love is patient, so therefore we can trust that God is patient. God never tires of waiting – waiting for the prodigal children to return, waiting for the children of the world to discover forgiveness in place of revenge.

More than that, God is love, and love is kind. Paul tells us that love is kind. Why do so many humans want to blame God for disasters and sickness rather than believing that God is kind and is on the side of the sufferers rather than on the side of the disease? If anyone can believe that 'God is love, God is kind, and God loves me,' then they can wait more patiently till it becomes possible for God my friend to bring the suffering to an end.

Again, connecting John and Paul, we read that God who is love is not envious, boastful, arrogant or rude. Down the centuries there have been stories of people who aimed too high, only to be brought down for their arrogance. But perhaps there was nothing personal in the downfall: fly too near the sun and your wings will melt, but the heat was not put there to catch anybody out. God does not boast of the beauty of creation; rather it is that most people in the world do not believe God exists.

God who is love does not insist on his own way, we may conclude from John added to Paul. We humans can spend long and agonised hours praying to find out exactly what God wants us to do, when sometimes we need to make up our own minds for the best, and trust that God will go along with our decision. God may have a blueprint, but it is flexible. It has to be, given our waywardness, but in the end love will triumph.

God who is love is not irritable or resentful, but rather is always patient and kind. God does not have a short fuse. God does not rejoice in wrongdoing, but rejoices in the truth. God bears all things, believes all things, hopes all things, endures all things.

God is love that never ends.

If as followers of Jesus we believe that God is love, then there is a ready answer to any non-believer who says God does not exist. Love certainly exists: we can observe love in action in nearly every situation in the world.

FORTY-SEVEN

More than

Ephesians 3:20, 21

Listen again to what Paul writes to his friends in Ephesus. 'Now to him who by the power at work within us is able to accomplish abundantly far more than all we can ask or imagine . . .' God can accomplish not just more than we ask, but *abundantly* more; not just abundantly more, but abundantly *far* more than we ask; not just more than we do ask, but more than we *can* ask, and even more than we can imagine.

If we search our hearts and our memories, as the years go by most of us could give examples of overflowing gifts from God that were beyond expectation. One that comes to mind from the story of Jesus himself is that of the thief who was crucified beside Jesus who was promised Paradise that same day (Luke 23:43). Not only was Paradise with Jesus a gift beyond the thief's hopes and dreams, but think of the millions of poor sinners over the centuries who have found the courage to believe in God's mercy through hearing about that small exchange between Jesus and the thief. It is never too late to ask for forgiveness, and the poor thief was the one who dared to ask.

There is a centuries-old prayer of the Church that echoes Paul's words to the Ephesians. Nowadays it has its place as the opening prayer on the twenty-seventh Sunday of the year, but for centuries, well before the Reformation, it was the Collect prayer for the eleventh Sunday after Pentecost. The Church of England retained it also, as the Collect for the tenth Sunday after Trinity. Here is a translation from the Latin original as it appears in a daily missal dating from 1934:

> Almighty and everlasting God, who out of the abundance of your loving kindness, in answering the prayer of the one who calls upon you, are wont to go beyond the desires and the hopes of the suppliant: do please pour forth upon us your mercy; forgive us those sins on account of which our conscience is afraid; and endow us with those good things for which our prayer ventures not to ask.

It is a strange sensation, to be asking for things we do not venture or dare to ask for. I can think of someone, a friend of mine, who secretly yearned to be a writer, but he had no expectation that it would ever happen. So far he has written and published 25 books. This sort of answer to hidden good desires can happen, and the prayer and the words of Paul tell us we can surely be bold in our prayers for the desires of our hearts.

However, the most usual way in which God goes ahead of our prayers and our desires lies in having God for a personal friend. To feel loved, to feel related, to feel forgiven over things happening that would otherwise cause us distress, to feel we have a place in the heart of the gospel story – all these and more are beyond what we have any right to. Our life could be over at any time, but whenever we die, we will die forgiven.

FORTY-EIGHT

You will be forgiven

Luke 6:37

'Forgive, and you will be forgiven,' said Jesus, along with, 'Do not judge, and you will not be judged; do not condemn, and you will not be condemned.' It almost seems that there are two ways to become a 'saint among the saints' and to enter the kingdom of heaven. The glorious way is the way of heroism in the face of persecution and difficulties of all sorts. The back door to heaven – the humbler way – is simply to stop judging other people, to stop condemning them, and to forgive them. That humbler way, just as much guaranteed by Jesus as the glorious way, is nonetheless a way to avoid being judged by Jesus when he comes again. It is a way much to be recommended.

This is not, however, a matter simply of avoiding the final judgement when we die. What Jesus tells us to do has an immediate effect here and now. Either we live in a world of condemnation and judging, or we may choose to live in world of forgiveness, non-condemnation and no judgement of other people's motives. The marvellous result of living without judging is that other people's judgements of me just bounce off me, no matter whether their judgements are kind or cutting. I am not living in that world. I am living in the world of Jesus, in the world of truth, where I am already forgiven.

Some people, it is true, are obliged or expected to make judgements of a sort. Parents have standards for their children to live up to; teachers always want their pupils to use their memories and understanding and make progress; judges in court have to insist on good laws being kept, and to deal with the persons who flout the law. But parents, teachers and judges do not have to condemn their children, their students or criminals. Parents love their children while they try to correct their children's behaviour. Teachers can refuse to give up on their students, and judges can hope for redemption for the prisoners.

Jesus did not come into the world to condemn, but to save. Think if you will about Jesus and the woman arrested when she was found committing adultery. He never condemned the woman: 'Neither do I condemn you,' is what he told her. He added, 'Go your way, and from now on do not sin again,' but there is no reason to believe he would not forgive again if she were to sin again (John 8:3-11).

Another wonderful result of forgiving all others and thus being forgiven oneself is that effort towards doing good becomes easier. I am not starting each day with the burden of what I did wrong or badly yesterday. On the contrary, yesterday is all forgiven, and I can put my whole heart into doing the best I can today. Each of us can say, 'I am God's beloved son' or 'I am God's beloved daughter,' regardless of what anybody else thinks of me, and then drop all charges against God's other daughters or sons. Why not leave it to God to understand everyone else's motives?

FORTY-NINE

'... your holy servant Jesus'

Acts 4:27-30

Reading through the story of the very early Church in Luke's Acts of the Apostles, we can be startled by turns of phrase that nowadays sound strange to us. Here in today's reading we have the infant Christian community praying to God in thanksgiving for the release from arrest of the apostles Peter and John. Praying to God, they thank God for his healing and for the signs and wonders worked by God's holy servant Jesus, and for the signs worked by the apostles in the name of God's holy servant Jesus. We do not usually think about Jesus as the servant of God, but clearly that was the way Jesus was thought of in that early prayer.

There is a long history behind the giving of that title to Jesus. As Jesus' public life went on, his closest disciples were beginning to recognise what Jesus himself knew already – that he was gradually fulfilling the prophecies in the Scriptures concerning the Messiah, the Christ who was to come. The clearest ones were the prophecies about the Shepherd, about the King of David's line, about the Son of Man, and about the Prophet like Moses that Moses said would come to complete Moses' work at some future time. There was, however, one line of prophecy that the disciples studiously avoided finding, though Jesus knew it very well, and in fact it was very clearly written in the Scriptures: the Messiah would be the obedient Servant of God, would give his life in service, and would be killed before he triumphed (see, for example, Isaiah 53).

The apostle Peter was inspired to see Jesus as the Christ, but then immediately resisted the consequence, which was that Jesus would have to go to Jerusalem and be killed for teaching about God's love and forgiveness (Mark 8:27-33). Jesus knew he would have to put his life on the line rather than weaken the message he had received from God his Father. He was a messenger, bound in duty to deliver his message; he was the Son of God, who came from God and who alone knew God through and through. Unless Jesus gave the world the truth about God, who else, before or after, would be able to reassure us sinners? The prophecies about the Christ having to suffer are written large in the Scriptures, but nobody – only Jesus – had eyes open to see.

Until, that is, the resurrection of Jesus, when the hearts of the disciples were warmed and consoled; then at last they could see all over the Scriptures where it was said to be necessary for the Christ to suffer, and thus to enter his glory. That must be the reason why Jesus is so freely called the holy servant of God in this prayer of the early Church. However, the more it dawned on the disciples that the whole life, death and resurrection of Jesus placed him at the right hand of God, the more the title of 'holy servant of God' for Jesus faded into the background again, even though the truth behind it did not fade.

Incidentally, this waxing and waning of the title of 'servant' for Jesus is one of the indications that Luke used old records and memories to write his history. By the time he came to write the Acts of the Apostles, that title was no longer in everyday use for Jesus.

FIFTY

About Bar'abbas

Acts 3:14, 15

So many of the details mentioned in the Gospels and in the rest of the New Testament look innocent, but in fact they have deeper, unexpected meanings for the one who wrote in the first place. Take Barabbas, for instance. I am sure that was his name, but Mark and the other evangelists could see a startling significance in the name when they had time to reflect.

'Bar' means 'son of', just as Mark told us when Jesus, on the way to Jerusalem, cures the blind man Bartimaeus the son of Timaeus (Mark 10:46-52). There is a striking contrast between Barabbas, the man in prison with the rebels who has committed murder during an insurrection, and Jesus who only gives life. Barabbas is a slang name: it means 'son of his *abba*', that is 'son of his daddy' – but nobody knows who his daddy was. He is illegitimate. Jesus, on the other hand, is known to the Gospel writer to be Son of God, whom he calls his *Abba*.

Not long after the death and resurrection of Jesus, Peter and John cure a lame man who is begging at the Beautiful Gate of the temple (Acts 3:1-10). This causes such a stir that Peter is able to stand up and make a speech about the fact that he and John have not worked this miracle by their own power, but only by invoking the name of Jesus. Peter then reproaches the populace of Jerusalem for choosing a murderer, Barabbas, to be released when they could have asked freedom for Jesus, 'the Author of life': 'You rejected the holy and Righteous One and asked to have a murderer given to you.'

Already, only weeks after the death of Jesus, Peter's titles for Jesus are such as belong to the Messiah, and even beyond that. Jesus is not only life-giving here and now; he is the very 'Author of life' ('all things were created through him' – John 1:3). He is the Holy One, whom God promised in Psalm 16:10 would never see corruption. Peter makes the connection between Jesus risen on the third day and the new life available for those who would believe in Jesus. Barabbas was a rebel and a murderer, but Jesus was the obedient one, who taught the truth from God about justification and righteousness.

So the name of the prisoner preferred to Jesus by the high priest is a coincidence, but it has upside-down references to Jesus as the exact opposite of Barabbas. Mark wrote his Gospel using the often-told accounts of the disciples who had known Jesus before and after his death and resurrection. Mark wrote it in a time of persecution, and a number of his expressions are upside down, like the tree that withers compared with the tree of the cross which does not, or the temple that will not have a stone left upon a stone, compared with the temple built of living stones that Peter will describe. His readers would understand the references.

FIFTY-ONE

Peter fears the waves

Matthew 14:28-33

People suffering from the scourge of epilepsy are taught to be afraid of open fire and of deep water. Even in the early stage of the disease, petit mal, they can have a sudden bout of complete unawareness of their surroundings: they might freeze with a hand over a gas or an electric fire and not feel anything till it is too late; they might take mouthfuls of water while swimming and be unaware that they are drowning.

The Gospels tell us that the apostle Peter had a crisis with an open fire, and also a crisis where he was in danger of drowning in the sea. The open fire was in the court of the high priest, where Peter had followed the troop of soldiers and servants who had arrested Jesus. Mark says Peter was warming himself at the fire (Mark 14:67). Luke says it was the light from the fire that made Peter recognisable by the maid (Luke 22:56). Peter was not prepared to own up to who he was.

There are more incidents that could link Peter to what happens in a case of epilepsy – not that he was suffering from the disease, but that the disease shows up certain similarities, in a spiritual sense, to Peter's story. When he, James and John came down from the mountain where Jesus was transfigured, there was the father of a boy with epilepsy, asking for a cure for his son. Jesus said to his other disciples, who had been unable to cure the boy, 'This kind [of spirit] can only come out through prayer' (Mark 9:29). It is surely noticeable later on that Peter had not prayed before he entered into temptation at the courtyard of the high priest. Instead of praying, 'I believe; help my unbelief!' like the father of the epileptic boy (Mark 9:24), Peter had let Jesus do the praying while he himself went to sleep (Mark 14:32-41).

Even the dramatic fall and meaningless cries of a sufferer from epilepsy are mimicked in the story of Peter in crisis: he began to curse and swear that he did not know this man Jesus of Nazareth who had just been arrested (Mark 14:71). Meaningless words from Peter, who knew and loved Jesus as well as anyone did.

In our case, in the twenty-first century, there is still a spirit around that can render us unable to own up in public that we are followers of Jesus: it is the spirit of fear. Jesus tells us time and time again not to be afraid. He said moments before Peter stepped out of the boat, 'Take heart, it is I; do not be afraid' (Matthew 14:27). Peter had enough faith at that moment to venture onto the waves, but as soon as he noticed the strong wind his unbelief overtook him. He did, though, have the sense to pray a short, sharp prayer of belief in the presence of Jesus. 'Lord, save me!' he cried, and Jesus reached out his hand and caught him.

The moral of the story is that we would do better to pray before a crisis rather than to repent afterwards.

FIFTY-TWO

Temple curtain torn

Mark 15:37-8

When Jesus breathed his last on the cross, Mark tells us that he gave a loud cry, and the curtain of the temple was torn in two, from top to bottom. To realise the significance of this statement we could start from a long distance away, far from Jerusalem.

Imagine we are here in northern Europe at the time when Jesus was still a child, and we want to get as close as possible to the throne of God upon the Earth. We would have to travel all the way across Europe by land or sea, or both, and find our way to the Holy Land. The journey would be difficult and dangerous. Then, having reached the Holy Land, we would have to find our way to Jerusalem.

Having reached Jerusalem, we would find the whereabouts of the temple fairly easily, since it must have been the biggest non-military building in the whole city, the temple that took 46 years to build. We would be allowed to enter the temple as far as the court of the Gentiles, and that would be that. Even a Jewish woman would only be allowed to enter into one more court, and that would be that for her. A Jewish man could enter one more court, and could share that with the (male) priests. But the Holy Place within the final court was an inner sanctum which only the priests could enter and carry out sacred duties.

Between the Holy Place and the Holy of Holies was a curtain, an opaque veil, shrouding the figure of the cherubim whose wings were the throne of God, where the invisible God dwelt with human beings. Only the high priest or his delegate would dare to pass through that curtain to offer incense.

Hence the significance of the curtain being torn in two from top to bottom: thanks to Jesus having sacrificed his life to proclaim the unconditional love and forgiveness of God his *Abba*, the way is now open for any child of God, any brother or sister of Jesus, to come into the presence of God without an appointment, without an introduction. Tearing down the curtain cost Jesus his lifeblood, and it is always thanks to Jesus that we have such free access to our loving God: no need to journey miles, no need to reach the Holy Land or Jerusalem, no barriers of gender or qualifications.

We are all first-generation children of God, and God is our *Abba*, not just our creator or the father of the human race; he is not a distant God. Like little children of God, we will never find our Father too busy to listen to us. Every one of us can say, 'I will never find my Father too busy to listen to me.' The throne of God is there in the heart of each and every one of us, and the door to it is open.

FIFTY-THREE

Grateful leper

Luke 17:11-19

Ten lepers, keeping their distance from Jesus as he approaches a certain village on his way to Jerusalem, call out to him, 'Jesus, Master, have mercy on us!' Jesus does have mercy. He sends them off to show themselves to the priests; they set out, and on the way they find themselves to be clean, healed of their disease. However, only one of them turns back; he praises God with a loud voice, kisses the ground before Jesus and thanks him. He is a foreigner, a Samaritan, and Jesus asks to know where the other nine are, since all ten were healed.

Jesus' final words to the healed man are surprising: 'Get up and go on your way; your faith has made you well.' The man shows faith in Jesus as the source of healing that could only come from God. He has faith; the other nine have not. His gratitude is the sign of his faith.

Gratitude is a key to many things in the world of Jesus. One could almost identify gratitude as the greatest of the virtues and ingratitude as the origin of all sin. The life of Jesus is centred round 'as the Father loves me' and his own desire to thank his Father by doing the will of the Father at all times. Subsequently, we as followers of Jesus are to love one another in gratitude for the total love that Jesus has shown to us. We are not expected to love God 'from cold', as it were, but as a thanksgiving for gifts received and for the love behind the gifts.

It is quite easy to read gratitude/ingratitude into the biblical account of Adam and Eve and the origin of sin (Genesis 3). There they were, not a care in the world, with a whole paradise of flowers, and trees by the thousands. Instead of being grateful for the thousands, they become suspicious of God for telling them not to touch one dangerous tree. 'What is God keeping from us?' Ingratitude leads to lack of trust. Jesus will in his day reverse that original sin by teaching us gratitude, and to trust God as his *Abba* and ours.

When we reflect of an evening on the doings of the day, it is far better to count the blessings of the day before recalling all the things that went wrong. If we start with the disappointments, the mistakes and the negative events of the day, we are much more likely to end up in depression and spiritual desolation: the good and happy moments will be submerged and forgotten. Every day has its happy moments, where things – perhaps surprisingly – turn out well. One psychologist known to me encourages everyone first to recall in the evening three things in the past day that went well or happily. Sometimes it is a struggle to remember three, but the effort to recall them changes the day's memories from negative to positive.

A good and useful practice is to write a one-line record of the blessings of the day, and then to add to it each day, listing one or two things that went well. Over the weeks that follow, the list grows and grows, and the blessings can be recalled any time we are beginning to feel sorry for ourselves and to think nobody loves us.

FIFTY-FOUR

Walking on water

Mark 6:48

Living in faith is like walking on water. At first, whoever wants to believe in God will feel as if they are walking on water, as Jesus walked on the lake, coming towards his disciples at the time they were straining at the oars in the boat against an adverse wind. Faith means praying to God while half the world does not believe that God exists. Faith means believing in a loving God while half the world concentrates on all that goes wrong in the world and questions how there could be a loving God if he lets so many things go wrong, so many people suffer. Faith is like trusting in something or someone who may or may not be there at all.

I know someone who was invited as a child to talk to Jesus all the time, when he was not talking to anyone else. His schoolteacher suggested that instead of talking to himself all the time, why not tack 'Jesus' on to the end of every sentence to turn it into a shared thought, a thought shared with Jesus instead of just a lonely thought. He tried it out; it became a habit, and he still does it 50 years later. One immediate good result was that unworthy thoughts, such as thoughts of jealousy or dislike of other children, had a natural check. He knew he could not expect Jesus to agree, and it became more important to keep Jesus as a friend than to give free rein to his unpleasant instincts.

The general principle is to act as if God is real and available in our own heart, and to be faithful to that until such time as it is seen, understood and felt to be true. Provided the image we have is that of God as love, we will be in touch with a meaning for the world and for the universe that is positive and constructive. Jesus the image of God was a carpenter, not a demolition expert. There are huge sorrows in the world, and many of them are caused by people who do not believe in love. Many more, of course, just happen in nature, but why not accept that nature takes its course and that God is aware of the suffering but is unable to heal it and put everything right until the right time comes.[8] I would rather have a God who knows exactly what I am feeling, who loves me, and who will rescue me in time, than to have no god at all.

---

8. See Number 62 (page 132) for more about this.

There are big disasters every year, and where is God? God is in the love, dedication and generosity of the rescue workers and the local or international government workers trying to put the city or the situation together again. God is in the sheer courage of the survivors helping one another to stay alive. God is in the doctors and psychiatrists trying to put back together the lives of children who have been abused. God is in the parents and teachers working for a better world. Wherever love is, there is God. As long as love exists, God exists. To say there is no God is to say that there is no love.

Oftentimes it happens that acting as if God is love and God exists and God knows just what I am going through all the time can lead to moments of sudden insight and clarity of understanding. These occasions are gifts beyond anything I could have worked out for myself. These moments of great consolation can only be gifts from God. Faith thereby becomes knowledge. But a lifetime of faith even with no great felt sense of God's presence is still more worth living than a life with no purpose.

FIFTY-FIVE

One day at a time

1 Kings 17:7-16

We have heard the story of Elijah and the widow of Zarephath. The rains had stopped falling and the rivers were dried up when God told Elijah to go to Zarephath; there a widow would put him up for as long as he needed. Elijah set out, and when he arrived he saw a widow gathering sticks for a house fire. He asked her to give him some water in a vessel so that he could drink, and then he asked her to bake him a scone for something to eat.

Her reply was startling: in her house she had only a handful of meal in a jar and a little oil in a jug. She was gathering sticks to make a fire so as to bake a scone for her son and for herself. Then there was nothing more in the larder, and she and her son would die unless the rains came back.

Elijah was confident that the rains would come back because he believed his marching orders were from God, and God was not sending him to die of thirst. So he asked the widow to bake a little cake for him, and then something for her son and herself. She did this, knowing him, I suppose, to be a holy man. The wonderful thing then was that the handful of meal in the jar and the small jug of oil lasted not just for that one day, but it was renewed each day until the day when the rains came back. Every day they woke up to find enough meal in the jar and enough oil in the jug.

We in the twenty-first century may feel that this story of Elijah and the widow of Zarephath is rather tall, as stories go. We were not there at the time, and we do not know exactly what happened, but there is a parable or a lesson contained in the story, a parable that goes like this: 'When you think you may not have enough resources for tomorrow, but you have enough for today, concentrate on today and trust in God for tomorrow. Do not let worries about tomorrow spoil what you can do today.' There is a saying quoted by Taoiseach Bertie Ahern when addressing the House of Commons: 'There is no greater mistake than to do nothing because you can only do a little.'

If that sounds rather secular and not particularly Christian, then think of Jesus on the hillside with five loaves and two fishes. The apostles are saying, 'What is the use of five loaves and two fishes among so many thousands of hungry people?' Jesus, however, tells them to get on with it, to give out what they have. He must say the same to us Christians when we look at our own smallness and weakness, called upon as we are to make disciples of the whole world: 'Get on with what you have!'

FIFTY-SIX

Tree always in fruit

Mark 11:12-14

It always seems strange to hear a story about Jesus doing something negative, like this story about when he is walking with his closest disciples back into Jerusalem from the village of Bethany where he has stayed the night. The story as written in Mark's Gospel, probably told to Mark by Peter, has Jesus feeling hungry. Seeing in the distance a fig tree in leaf, Jesus goes up to the tree to see whether he would find anything on it in the way of edible fruit. But the tree has nothing but leaves, since it is not the season for fruit. Jesus then says the tree's days are numbered, and nobody will obtain fruit from it again.

We have to remember that Jesus is in his own land, entering his own capital city. He knows very well that figs are a summer fruit, and this is only March or April as it is coming up to Passover time. He knows he will find only leaves, and nothing to ease his hunger. Jesus is acting here as a prophet acts, creating a scene with a lesson – a visual aid for the message he wants to give his listeners: 'Trees may look fine, but they are only fruitful one month in twelve. I will give you a tree that will be fruitful in all seasons, every month of the year, so that you need never go hungry.'

The everlasting, ever-fruitful tree given to us by Jesus is the cross. It is surely no coincidence that the apostles Peter and Paul will talk about Jesus 'on the tree' when they mean 'on the cross'. Peter when he is on trial says, 'The God of our ancestors raised up Jesus, whom you had killed by hanging him on a tree' (Acts 5:30). To the convert Cornelius he says, 'They put him to death by hanging him on a tree' (Acts 10:39). Paul at Antioch in Pisidia says, 'When they had carried out everything that was written about him, they took him down from the tree and laid him in a tomb (Acts 13:29). Already Peter and the other disciples know the cross of Jesus as the tree of life that has been denied to humanity until now. The tree itself is something to cling to, and the fruit of the tree is the body and blood of Jesus, always readily available in any and every month of the year.

Ezekiel in his vision of the heavenly temple also saw trees: 'Their leaves will not wither nor their fruit fail, but they will bear fresh fruit every month, because the water for them flows from the sanctuary.

Their fruit will be for food, and their leaves for healing' (Ezekiel 47:12). That was the vision; the cross is the reality.

The Book of Revelation at the end of the Bible has the trees of life on the banks of the river of life in the New Jerusalem, again bearing fruit every month and with leaves for healing. This not now a prophecy, but a visionary description of what has already come true in Jesus. 'To everyone who conquers, I will give permission to eat from the tree of life that is in the paradise of God' (Revelation 2:7).

The Book of Deuteronomy holds that 'Anyone [criminal] hung on a tree is under God's curse.' (Deuteronomy 21:23). Paul writing to the Galatians sees here a sign of something that was reversed by the death of Jesus, to save and reassure all the rest of us (Galatians 3:13). Thanks be to God.

FIFTY-SEVEN

Holy Week and Easter

Mark 16:1, 2

Mark is the only one of the four Gospel writers who gives us a seven-day week that has its climax at the resurrection of Jesus. What is more surprising, Mark offers wide hints that this week of all weeks is the week in which God recreates all that was created in the beginning of time. The Book of Genesis starts with the seven days of creation, evening and morning, evening and morning, seven days from Saturday evening through to the following Saturday morning. Saturday is the holy day, the Sabbath. For Mark, the week runs from Sunday evening (Palm Sunday) through to Easter Sunday morning when the sun has already risen and Jesus, too, has risen. The holy day then becomes Sunday.

Mark's Holy Week runs like this. The **Sunday** we call Palm Sunday is the day Jesus enters Jerusalem and goes into the temple. There he looks around at everything, but because **it is already late** he goes out to Bethany with the 12.

On the following day, when they come from Bethany, Jesus is hungry. (1) On this day Jesus cleanses the temple. **And when evening comes**, Jesus and his disciples go out of the city.

In the morning as they pass by they see the fig tree withered. Jesus preaches in the temple at length. (2)

Jesus talks to the disciples about the stones of the temple. He ends with the parable about staying awake, whether **in the evening,** or at cockcrow, **or at dawn**, to be ready for the master's return. It is **now two days before** the Passover. (3) On the evening of that day Jesus is **at Bethany at supper** in the house of Simon the leper, when a woman anoints his head with very expensive ointment.

Next, **it is the first day** of the Feast of Unleavened Bread, when the Passover lamb is sacrificed. The disciples prepare the Passover meal. (4) **In the evening**, Jesus comes with the 12 to what we know as the Last Supper. There follows the prayer in the Garden of Gethsemane, and the arrest of Jesus. The high priest and the Sanhedrim try Jesus and condemn him. The apostle Peter denies that he ever knew Jesus.

As soon as it is morning the chief priests, the scribes and the whole council deliver Jesus to Pilate the Roman Governor. At nine o'clock in the morning they crucify him. (5) **When evening comes**, Jesus has died and his body is taken down and buried. The Jewish Sabbath is beginning.

In the morning it is still the Sabbath day, so movement is restricted. (6) **Saturday evening, the Sabbath ends**, but it is too late to allow the body to be anointed.

Sunday morning, **very early on the first day of the week**, when the sun has already risen, the women come to the tomb. The tomb is empty; Jesus is risen. (7)

FIFTY-EIGHT

From scarlet to white as snow

Isaiah 1:18

'. . . though your sins are like scarlet, they shall be like snow; though they are red like crimson, they shall become like wool.'

In the Western Christian Church we have just one feast of Saint Mary Magdalene each year, on 22 July. In the Eastern tradition three separate women are honoured, namely Mary Magdalene, Mary of Bethany the sister of Martha, and the unnamed 'woman who was a sinner' who washed the feet of Jesus with her tears and wiped them with her hair (Luke 7:36-50). In the Western Church we have tended to amalgamate the three stories and make them fit Mary Magdalene.

According to the Gospels, Mary Magdalene was one of the women who followed Jesus and who contributed to his mission from their own resources, enabling Jesus to give himself freely to the crowds who came to him. Luke tells us that Jesus had cured Mary Magdalene of 'seven demons' (Luke 8:2), which could well have led to her grateful assistance to Jesus. She is also named as one of the very few people attending at the foot of the cross during the hours Jesus hung on the cross.

Lastly, Mary Magdalene is the one who had a one-to-one meeting with Jesus on the morning he rose from the dead. That meeting is one of the most beautiful as well as the one of the most telling of all memories about Jesus: he only had to call her by her first name and she knew him immediately. Then she clung to his ankles as if never to let him go, which perhaps makes it a little easier for tradition to think she might be the same person as the sinner who washed his feet.

The story of Martha of Bethany and her sister Mary gives the impression that the family are quite comfortably off (Luke 10:38-42): they can offer hospitality to Jesus; the funeral of their brother Lazarus is quite a big affair (John 11). Mary is shown as a fairly contemplative person. It does seem unlikely that she has a record of sins like scarlet or like crimson.

There are two women who anointed Jesus: one is the woman with a bad reputation in the town, who anointed his feet with her tears; the other is also unnamed, who anointed his head with very expensive ointment at the supper in Bethany at the house of one Simon the leper. Through these two, Mary Magdalene has come to be thought of as a repentant sinner, freed and forgiven by Jesus and endlessly grateful.

Even when these women were unjustifiably seen as one and the same person – Mary Magdalene the repentant sinner – it is striking that the colour of vestment used by the priest at the Mass commemorating Mary was always white, not purple as if for Lent or Advent. The forgiveness Jesus brings renders the sinner as good as new, just as his works of healing make the sick completely better, as Luke the doctor tells us.

FIFTY-NINE

Two kinds of peace

John 14:27

'Peace I leave with you; my peace I give to you. I do not give to you as the world gives. Do not let your hearts be troubled, and do not let them be afraid.' The peace Jesus brings is different from another kind of peace, the kind the world gives. As far as that kind of peace is concerned, Jesus did not come to bring that. As he says on another occasion, 'Do you think that I have come to bring peace to the earth? No, I tell you, but rather division!' (Luke 12:51).

Jesus then goes on to talk about divisions within families that his teachings will bring to light. Instead of keeping available money secure within the family, one or more will listen to Jesus and then want to give a lot, or even everything they possess, to the poor – which will by no means please the rest of the family. Disciples of Jesus may no longer wish to follow in the family business or to uphold the family importance, to the sorrow of their parents. In effect, Jesus is teaching that everyone in the world is called to be a member of the one family – the human family, and also the divine family as children of God and brothers and sisters of Jesus himself.

The worldly view of 'family peace' means that nobody is to rock the boat and everything is to carry on as it has always carried on before. So long as the nuclear family is tightly knit and every member is of like mind, there will be peace as the world knows peace. Jesus is aware that following his teachings will disrupt family harmony – and village, town, city or national harmony – and will cause hurt both to his followers and to those they disappoint.

The peace Jesus brings is peace of heart. Ultimately it is the peace of knowing oneself to be forgiven by God. Each new day can then begin from a basis as firm as rock: if yesterday was handled well, I need not doubt it; if yesterday was badly handled, it is forgiven, and I can try again to love and serve God. Living to create a worldwide family of loving brothers and sisters is no easy task, and we can expect disappointments, opposition and hostility. However, that does not mean that we are wrong to be attempting such an ideal, any more than the crucifixion of Jesus meant he was wrong.

'Do not be afraid' in this context surely means, 'Do not lose confidence in the ideal just because so many people cannot or will not cooperate.' This enterprise is from God, and in the end it will succeed.

Paul's second letter to the Thessalonians ends with one of the most encouraging prayers wishing peace: 'Now may the Lord of peace himself give you peace at all times in all ways' (2 Thessalonians 3:16). The Lord of peace is Jesus himself, and this prayer is not for something that comes and goes depending on how we are doing, but it is for always and everywhere. That would explain why being forgiven at all times is the foundation of peace.

SIXTY

Only a few saved?

Revelation 21:15, 16

When someone asks Jesus, 'Will only a few be saved?' Jesus sidesteps and speaks instead about the need to enter by the narrow door, which only few want to do (Luke 13:23, 24). But surely he himself is about to enter by the narrow door, and it is not simply for his own satisfaction and self-congratulation. Jesus enters by the narrow door in order to widen it for the sinners he has come to save. His disciples are not about to have an easy passage either; they, too, will have to go by the narrow door, but the reason for doing so will be as servants and under-shepherds gathering together the sheep for the great Shepherd. They will not be striving for themselves only.

The last book of the Bible, the Revelation to John, encourages us to believe that in the end the number who get to heaven will not be just a few. First of all, there is the list of 144,000 servants of God marked with the seal on their foreheads; then a great multitude that no one could number, from all tribes and peoples and languages, standing before the throne and before the Lamb (Revelation 7:3-4).

Surprising, too, is the description in the same Book of Revelation of the dimensions of the new Jerusalem, the heavenly city. The heavenly Jerusalem is described as being 10,000 times the size of the greatest and most wicked city of the ancient world – Babylon. Babylon, according to the Greek historian Herodotus, was a square-shaped city, and each of the four city walls stretched 120 stadia. The new Jerusalem, according to John, is a square city, and each of the four walls stretches 12,000 stadia, or 100 times the length of Babylon's walls. Square that off and we have a picture of the new Jerusalem as 10,000 times the size of Babylon. A stadium measures one eighth of a mile, which is the length of a chariot-race stadium. The new Jerusalem is described in miles, therefore, as 1500 miles square, or 2,250,000 square miles in area. A lot of room, therefore, for a vision in the ancient world, where nothing like as many human beings lived compared with today.

Another strange statistic given in Revelation is that the city is as tall as it is long – that is to say 1500 miles tall! Probably we are not meant to think of a gigantic office block, but rather to picture the height of the highest building in the city. In Babylon this would have been the Ziggurat, or man-made mountain for purposes of worship – the Tower of Babel. In the new Jerusalem, however, there is no temple, for its temple is the Lord God Almighty and the Lamb.

Jesus allows us to think in terms of a family. God is our first-generation Father, and we are all brothers and sisters of Jesus, the Son of God. In a loving family every child is as precious as the next one. Jesus came to save us all: the family is not home until all the children are in their place at the table. Strict justice might not bring every last child into the new Jerusalem, but forgiveness could do it.

SIXTY-ONE

Peace comes back

Matthew 10:11-14

Jesus is instructing his 12 disciples as to how to conduct their mission when they are without his presence. One famous piece of advice he gives them is, 'If anyone will not welcome you or listen to your words, shake off the dust from your feet as you leave that house or town.' It is interesting to read in the Acts of the Apostles how Paul and the others interpreted his words in practice.

At Antioch in Pisidia Paul and Barnabas would meet with such heated opposition that they 'shook the dust off their feet in protest' against the townspeople and went on to the town of Iconium instead (Acts 13:51). Moreover, 'the disciples were filled with joy and with the Holy Spirit.' But that is not the end of the story for Antioch in Pisidia. Anyone reading through the story in Acts is sure to feel sympathy for the citizens of the town who did welcome Paul and Barnabas and their message. Were they to be deprived just because the important people in the town were deaf to the apostles?

The next chapter gives the answer. Paul and Barnabas went on to Lystra and Derbe, then doubled back by way of Iconium and Antioch to encourage the converts and establish elders to keep the new flocks together, and to tell them to expect persecution but not to be over-alarmed about it. So 'shaking off the dust' does not necessarily mean abandoning everyone in the town. Paul would be content with leaving a group or a 'church' within a town, even if the town as a whole was hostile.

Among the many important instructions Jesus gave the 12 disciples is one that is often forgotten by missionaries, teachers and parents: it concerns peace coming back. Jesus says, 'Whatever town or village you enter, find out who in it is worthy, and stay there until you leave. As you enter the house, greet it. If the house is worthy, let your peace come upon it; but if it is not worthy, let your peace return to you.'

So often, enthusiastic Christians, whether clergy or lay persons, can find themselves up against a brick wall of indifference. They themselves have peace of heart – or they thought they had until they met with the brick wall, or even with bitter opposition. In that case

Jesus seems to be saying, 'Your happiness and your peace of heart do not depend on how well you are received. Do not stay there hitting your head against the wall: go somewhere else, where there are people who would dearly love to hear your message. Do not lose your peace; let it come back to you.'

Go somewhere else, and do not reproach yourself over people who do not listen to you. God will look after them, as Paul told Timothy about Alexander the coppersmith who had done him great harm (2 Timothy 4:14). God will forgive them, no matter how long it takes. Paul looks forward to Christ's message reaching the whole people of the Jews before the end of things, even though up to now he can only convince some while he alienates others.

SIXTY-TWO

God is love

1 John 4:8

There are 70 or so books in the Bible, and the conclusion of the whole journey through the books and through the centuries is that God is love. Nobody dared to say that, nobody knew to say that, except at the end, the conclusion.

It is impossible to do justice to those three words (God is love) in one or in a million sermons. At this time we might investigate a couple of statements related to God and to love. The truth is, you cannot make God love you; you can only *let* God love you.

You cannot make God love you. God already loves you, and his love does not depend on your behaviour. To think that God will not love me if I do this or that is a mistake and a misunderstanding. Love will always love, no matter what we do. You or I might run away from God, fearing that every step is taking us further from God; but God is love and love is always the same. We have only to turn round to find that God's love never left us.

If I could make God love me by my good behaviour, or if I could stop God loving me by my bad behaviour, then I would be more powerful than God, which is nonsense.

There are two main hurdles we have to overcome in order to understand God's love. First, we come to understand that God loves us even though we are sinners. I can go through life as a forgiven sinner. Secondly, we try to understand that God loves us even though we are suffering. So many people turn away from God in times of suffering, as if the pain was aimed at them personally by someone they thought was a friend.

There are two things we say about God which seem to contradict one another: God is love, and God is all-powerful or almighty. One or the other has to be better understood, and the one to modify is 'all powerful'. Jesus more than once said that with God all things are possible; but then in his agony in the Garden of Gethsemane he prays, 'Abba, Father, for you all things are possible; remove this cup from me; yet not what I want, but what you want' (Mark 14:36). The love of Father and Son is still there, but what Jesus asks at that time is not possible there and then. Often, I am sure, God's love would answer our prayers of pleading if it were possible there and then, but now is not the time, and we must wait.

'You cannot make God love you; you can only *let* God love you.' Like Jesus, faced with a terrible end to his life on Earth, it is possible still to believe in a God who is love, who accompanies us moment by moment, and who will lead us through the valley of death, if only we will let him love us.

SIXTY-THREE

No taxes for the children

Matthew 17:24-7

Fishermen through the ages have been notorious for telling the size of 'the one that got away'. At first hearing, the story of Peter and Jesus and the coin in the fish's mouth sounds like another kind of fisherman's tale – too good to be true. In fact, however, the story is not there as a miracle story but as a teaching story. Take it step by step to grasp the message Matthew is relating.

Jesus has just returned with his disciples back to Capernaum, when the collectors of the temple tax approach Peter and ask, 'Does your teacher not pay the temple tax?' The question expects the answer 'No,' so that they could catch Jesus out for being too independent. Peter answers, 'Yes, he does,' but he does not know if that is the right answer. So when he goes home, he plans to relate the question to Jesus himself, to see what the right answer is.

Jesus gives Peter the answer before even being asked; he answers in a roundabout way, with another story: 'Simon,' says Jesus, 'from whom do kings of the earth take toll or tribute? From their children or from others? Think about it!' Simon Peter does not have to think for long. 'From others, of course; not from their own children,' he says. 'Then,' says Jesus, 'the children are free.' And therein is the first part of the lesson.

Peter and Jesus are children of God. The collectors of the temple tax are not entitled to collect from God's children a tax to pay for the house of God. Everyone else may be taxed, but not the children. An odd little story turns out to have an enormous significance: we know from Jesus that we are all first-generation children of God, so therefore any contribution God asks of us is not to be seen in the light of a tax. The children are free.

This leads us to the second half of the lesson. Although Jesus has said that he and Peter are free not to contribute the temple tax, he still does not want to give offence to the temple authorities and their tax collectors, who are not ready to understand Jesus' point of view in the matter. So he tells Peter to go to the lake and cast a hook, then to look in the mouth of the first fish he catches and he will find a coin that will be of value enough to pay the collectors and keep them happy. Jesus would never want them to think he is not bothered about the state of repair of the house of God.

The small story in Matthew's Gospel does not say that Peter did go fishing on this occasion, nor that he found in the first fish a coin big enough to pay for the two of them. Maybe he did, or maybe he had to keep fishing until he had a big enough catch to make money. This would seem to be the only time Simon Peter fished with a hook and line rather than with a net slung from his boat. This is a teaching story, not a miracle story. The message is a huge one: we are children of God, so God does not levy taxes on us. All the things our consciences ask us to do are voluntary contributions, to be done out of love for God our Father, not under threat.

SIXTY-FOUR

If they all went away...

Matthew 25:40

The parable Jesus tells about the king separating the sheep from the goats is unsettling, and I am sure it is meant to be so. 'Truly I tell you, just as you did it to one of the least of these who are members of my family, you did it to me.' And then: 'Truly I tell you, just as you did not do it to one of the least of these, you did not do it to me' (verse 45). In some ways this is consoling, to know that Jesus is present somehow in everyone we see or deal with, but his words pull us up short when we remember how shabbily we have treated so many people in our lifetime.

In the parable, the king is making a distinction between those who have always given love to others and those who have never, ever given unselfish love. We may wonder, is there anyone who ever went through life without a single thought, word or action in sympathy with anyone else? At best, our actions try to be consistently good but do not always end up virtuous. And villains like the thief crucified beside Jesus will have at least moments of honesty and goodwill: did he not take the food and drink from the mouths of his victims; did he not take the clothes from their backs; did he not rob strangers rather than his friends; did he not leave his victims feeling sick at heart; did he ever go to prison 'just visiting'? Yet he acknowledged his own guilt, and at the same time he declared Jesus' innocence. And then he was promised Paradise, to come that same day, in spite of seeming like a candidate to join the goats in the parable.

There is another consoling thought attached to the 'punchlines' of this parable of Jesus. Sometimes in moments of desolation any of us can feel left behind. To put it graphically, if everyone I know, if everyone in the world sailed away to heaven and left me behind as being not worth taking, where would Jesus be? He would be back here with me, because what the successful ones were doing to me – the least of the members of his family – they were doing to him, without realising what they were doing. Again graphically speaking, it looks now as though Peter at the gates of heaven would have to hold up the admissions until Jesus finally arrives with me. The story begins to sound like the shepherd going to look for the lost sheep and leaving the 99 others till he finds the missing one. Or like a brother in a big family who cannot rest while there is an empty place at the family table.

Maybe this is wrong, to use a frightening parable to find consolation, but to use it in this way is certainly effective. There are times in the lives of many people when they feel left behind, unsuccessful at whatever they have been aiming for, friendless, a failure, especially compared with their original ambitions and hopes of doing great things in their lives. They find themselves comparing unfavourably with just about everybody else. At such times it is good to remember that if I have been left behind, so has Jesus, and he does not seem to mind being there with me.

SIXTY-FIVE

Give without payment

Matthew 10:8; 18:23-35

Jesus is instructing his 12 disciples before sending them out as ambassadors for his own message. He tells them not to make people pay money for the wonderful truths they are bringing into their listeners' lives. They, the 12, did not have to pay Jesus for bringing the truth to them, so they should not attempt to make a profit on the enterprise by charging others for services rendered. Ultimately, God's love is free, and it would be very wrong to make anybody pay for it.

Future apostles have tried to keep to these words of Jesus as far as they could. Paul in his letters makes a point of saying he never cost his hearers a penny, but earned his living while he was among them by plying his trade as a tent-maker (Acts 20:34; 2 Thessalonians 3:8). Throughout history, missionaries have tried to avoid giving the impression that the truth can be bought: they may be poor and they may need looking after, but the message of good news comes free.

This notion of not making people pay has another meaning very dear to the heart of Jesus. It includes not making people pay for the wrongs they have done to us. It means, 'You have been forgiven freely, so forgive freely. Do not expect people to pay for what they did to you. Forgive them without any comeback, without any revenge in thought or action.'

One of the clearest parables of Jesus on this subject is the one in Matthew 18 about the unforgiving debtor. In the story, a king is owed a huge sum by a man who simply cannot pay the debt: something like billions of pounds sterling in today's money. The king lets the man off, so the debtor and his family are saved from penury and prison.

Then the freed man, a debtor no longer, goes out and starts to strangle another person who owes him a few hundred pounds – peanuts in comparison with his own former debt. The king when he hears about it is very angry and changes his mind about the big debt. The king demands payment. Does this mean Jesus is depicting God as someone who stops being loving if we stop being forgiving? Not that exactly. What it seems to mean is that we cannot believe in the forgiveness of sins if it means, 'I believe in the forgiveness of my sins, but I do not believe in the forgiveness of your sins or his sins or her sins.' For Jesus, I must either believe in the forgiveness of everybody's sins, or else live in a world where 'Pay up' is the rule. God is in the world of forgiveness; Jesus is in the world of forgiveness.

Why does my debt to God seem to be so huge compared with the small sum someone else owes me? Well, I owe God everything – sun, moon, stars, life, breath, family, friends, wisdom, fun, beauty, everything; the things I expect other people to pay up for are very small by comparison.

SIXTY-SIX

All is well?

Romans 8:28

'We know that all things work together for good for those who love God, who are called according to his purpose.' So says the apostle Paul, writing to the Christians in Rome before he went there himself (Romans 8:28). Paul is confident that the Roman brothers and sisters will have experienced the same as he has experienced himself, namely that when good things happen and when unfortunate things happen, the same end result comes to pass: God's Providence looks after everything.

The happy ending does not just come about because we love God. We cannot love God from cold; at least, God does not expect us to love him blindly. First, God wants us to know ourselves loved, in the world and the whole universe of created things, in the way Jesus and the prophets and teachers of the Bible open up to us, and in the many gifts that God has given to each and every one of us – no two people exactly the same. With a bright consciousness of how many gifts are mine, I can begin to trust that the giver of so much is not going to abandon me.

The holy woman Julian of Norwich wrote the famous lines: 'It is true that sin is the cause of all this pain. But all shall be well and all shall be well, and all manner of thing shall be well.'[9] Modern translators tend to put it this way: 'It is going be all right, it is going to be all right; everything is going to be all right.'[10] There is a startling version of Julian's words in a recent song to come out of Minneapolis, Minnesota: 'Everything always is, always was, always will be all right.'[11] The argument of the song is that if everything will be all right, then we are in a story with a happy ending even though the present may seem difficult to resolve into happiness. And it also follows, the song argues, that even the past is part of a story that will have a happy ending, if you accept what the lady Julian saw in her visions. The singer/songwriter then adds, 'If here and now everything is not all right, then it means we haven't yet reached the end!'[12]

---

9. James Walsh (trans), *The Revelations of Divine Love of Julian of Norwich*, Wheathampstead: Anthony Clarke Books, 1973, chapter 32, p.98.
10. Clifton Wolters (trans), *Julian of Norwich: Revelations of Divine Love,* Penguin Classics, 1966, chapter 32, p.109.
11. Wookiefoot, 'Always is' from the album *Be fearless and play.*
12. Wookiefoot, 'Always is'.

All is well?

This does depend on goodwill towards God, admittedly. There is a certain amount of self-abandonment required, and trust that God is capable of bringing about happy endings. Most people who are conscious of life as a gift – a gift from God – will be able to tell you of situations that looked very black but turned out to be surprisingly wonderful: for example, an illness that took a person out of one job situation into another career which turned out to be much better than the one left behind. An extreme case might be something like this: an accident eventually leads to someone becoming a Paralympic champion who would never have been recognised otherwise.

Of course, in the end, the apostle Paul is asking us to believe in a happy ending even though we are dying, as we all have to die some day. But in the meantime it is a great help and a blessing to be able to remind ourselves of the message from Minnesota: 'Everything always is, always was, always will be all right.' If everything isn't yet all right, that's because it isn't yet the end.

SIXTY-SEVEN

God shows no partiality

Galatians 2:6

This saying is used by Paul more than once, mainly to assert that he is as good an apostle as any other. In the Old Testament, in the Book of Deuteronomy and in the second Book of Chronicles, the same statement is used to indicate the fairness of God as a judge between people (Deuteronomy 10:17; 2 Chronicles 19:7). God will never accept a bribe to favour one side rather than another in a dispute.

Paul writing to the Romans, and the apostle Peter speaking to the convert Cornelius, use the same saying to indicate that God is happy to accept pagans for conversion and baptism, to become followers of the Way of Jesus (Romans 2:11; Acts 10:34). The Holy Spirit has clearly been at work, the apostles reckon, and the memories of those who knew Jesus as a preacher and teacher would agree that Jesus often found greater faith among the pagans he met than in his own Jewish people.

Were not the Jewish people God's favourites from centuries back? The shift in the apostles' stance indicates a new understanding. Yes, the Jewish people were chosen long ago to bring the worship of the one God to the whole world, and that is what they have done. Paradoxically, it came about through the life, death and resurrection of Jesus: now the whole world may find God by becoming followers of the Way.

I think there is a more personal way to understand how God does not show partiality. Again, it is best understood through the eyes of Jesus. Put it this way: God has no favourites. Like a good human father or mother, God does not think more highly of any one of his children ahead of any other one. I know parents often find one or other of their children easier to get on with than the others – easier to talk to, easier to understand. But in a crisis, human parents will not allow any one of their children to be left behind – all the more so if we believe God is love and we are God's children.

There is another very telling phrase on this matter: 'All my love'. No matter how many children there may be in a family, a mother writing letters to each of them can sign off truthfully, 'All my love, Mum.' If a mother can give all her love to each of however many children she may have brought into the world, then surely God can match that?

And yet, what a wonderful conclusion may be drawn from all this. At first it might seem a pity that I may not count myself as God's favourite child, that God does not show partiality to me. But turn the idea inside out and it means that God does not favour anyone else above me. God is as concerned and as full of love regarding me as he is regarding anyone else on Earth, past, present or to come. There is no such thing as a partial presence of God: where God is, God is simply and wholly there. And where God is, love is.

SIXTY-EIGHT

Firstborn

Hebrews 12:23

This amazing passage from the letter to the Hebrews seems to take it for granted that every member of the Christian faith shares the privileged position of the firstborn in a family. Not only are we brothers and sisters of Jesus the firstborn Son, but in and with him we also share the full inheritance. It is not only males who are included, but also the females of the family, who share the same. A rather clumsy word is used today quite frequently: we are co-heirs with Christ.

In our present life we do not know very clearly what our heavenly inheritance will be like; we can only guess, and guess in hope that it will finally satisfy our restless hearts. But there is a blessing contained in the word 'inheritance' that can make an enormous difference in our present life if we fully appreciate its meaning. An inheritance is something that comes to us; an inheritance does not depend on my worthiness: I cannot earn heaven; heaven is a gift. My life is not meant to be a desperate, endless effort to be considered good enough for God to be pleased: it results in depression every time I fail, and it results in pride if I think myself better than other people.

There are many passages in the Gospels that warn us not to count on earning our inheritance. The elder brother of the prodigal son is a prime example (Luke 15:11-32): he has been working in the family field year after year with very little thanks from his father. His father assures him, 'All that is mine is yours.' The other son is also precious, even though he has not earned anything. The prodigal one planned to say to his father, 'Treat me like one of your hired hands,' but the father does not let him get that far in his speech. He has the best robe brought out, a ring for the finger, and all the other privileges he can think of. Nothing is too good for the one who has come back.

The story Jesus told of the labourers in the vineyard contains the same warning (Matthew 20:1-16). All the labourers receive the same reward – one denarius for one day's manual labour – even though some of them have worked for 12 hours that day, where the latecomers have only worked for one hour. The landowner is generous, and chooses to give everyone the same: he reckons it is not the fault of the latecomers that nobody hired them all day long. This is not exactly a matter of inheritance, but Jesus does seem to be teaching that we need not expect a higher place in heaven just because we think we have worked harder than other people around us. Life for a Christian is an opportunity to thank our generous God for a gift we do not have to earn.

The same message comes through from the story of the Pharisee and the tax collector at prayer in the temple (Luke 18:10-14). The Pharisee is relying on how many rules he has kept; the tax collector is relying on the mercy of God. With the same message in mind, Jesus wants us not to add up our score of prayers said, fasts kept and alms given so as not to fall into the trap of thinking either, 'I have earned heaven,' or, 'I am a total failure'. We are to keep trying peacefully, leaving the matter of inheritance to God's generosity.

SIXTY-NINE

All sins forgiven

Hebrews 10:18

The letter to the Hebrews quotes the prophet Jeremiah as saying God 'will remember their sins and their lawless deeds no more' once the new covenant arrives (Hebrews 10:17; see Jeremiah 31:34). Where there is forgiveness of these, continues the letter, there is no longer any offering for sin. What it comes to is this: when all sins have been forgiven, there can be no more sin offerings (which is how the Jerusalem Bible puts it). No need to go to the temple any more to obtain forgiveness for sins, since the sins have already been forgiven.

The early Christian Church had a problem with the forgiveness of sins. All sins were forgiven in baptism, and for a time it seemed as though nobody would ever sin again once they had sincerely undergone baptism. But what about the sad fact of relapsing, of falling back into sin? This quotation from Hebrews seems to say that the lapses after baptism have also been forgiven, that Jesus brought from God permanent forgiveness along with the new covenant, which is for the forgiveness of sins.

There can be no doubt that Jesus in his public ministry forgives people first and then looks for improvement or repentance afterwards. Take Zacchaeus, for example – the little man who climbs the tree in order to have a good sight of Jesus passing by (Luke 19:1-10). If Jesus were to volunteer to stay at Zacchaeus' house provided he promised to obey every single law of Moses, the offer could not be accepted. Even more so, if Jesus were to make the offer conditional on the tax collector giving half his money to the poor and promising to pay back fourfold anyone he has cheated, Zacchaeus would run a mile. But Jesus starts with forgiveness, and the repentance follows.

Jesus eating with sinners does not ask for conversion first. When he says to the paralysed man let down through the roof, 'Son, your sins are forgiven' (Mark 2:5), Jesus does not make any conditions, nor with the woman who is a sinner: 'Your sins are forgiven' (Luke 7:48). Jesus is saying that sins have been forgiven, not by him but by God his Father, and Jesus is bringing that good news to those who are willing to hear it. Jesus' story of the prodigal son gives a clear picture of what

God is like (Luke 15:11-32), in that the father of the prodigal forgives the boy when he comes back, before he comes back, as soon as he arrives on the horizon, long awaited, and indeed before he ever went away. The sinner is never not forgiven, and that is what God is like. And that is at the heart of the new covenant.

Jesus died rather than describe his Father any other way. His worst enemies were those who did not believe in the forgiveness of sinners' sins, who did not believe sinners were already forgiven and only needed telling so from God to enable them to live a different kind of life. The Apostles' Creed asks us to say, 'I believe in the forgiveness of sins' – that is, not just my sins, but your sins as well, and everybody's sins. Jesus did not die to placate God his Father for our sins: God did not and does not want placating; he only wants to forgive.

SEVENTY

'Immediately'

Mark 1:10, 12, 18, 20, 21, 23, 28-30, 42, 43

People reading the Gospel of Mark are usually puzzled by the number of times he uses the word 'immediately', wondering why he does it. There are something like 52 times Jesus goes here or there, or this or that happens 'immediately'. Usually the Greek word Mark uses is *euthus*, just sometimes *parachrema*, but usually *euthus*.

Was Mark just a poor writer, they wonder, cobbling sentences together, or was he purposely giving a sense of urgency to the start of Jesus' public life, as Jesus' days of freedom were numbered?

The real reason, I think, goes like this: *euthus*, as an adverb, means 'immediately' or 'straightway' or 'straight away'. But the same word is also used as an adjective, meaning 'straight' or 'direct'. In verse 3 of the first chapter of Mark, he quotes the prophets Malachi and Isaiah as saying,

> See, I am sending my messenger ahead of you,
> who will prepare your way; (Malachi 3:1)
> the voice of one crying out in the wilderness,
> 'Prepare the way of the Lord,
> make his paths straight.' (Isaiah 40:3)

And the word for 'straight' is the adjective belonging to *euthus*.

So Mark is telling us that John the Baptist was the messenger who fulfilled the prophesy of Isaiah and made the paths straight for Jesus. Hence Jesus could go 'straight here' and 'straight there', 52 times, rather than having to go about his mission in a roundabout way.

What was it that John the Baptist did that prepared the way and made it straight for Jesus to go forward? What John did was to call people to be baptised, to admit that they were sinners (Mark 1:4). Then they were ready to receive the Spirit of adoption offered by Jesus. 'He will baptise you with the Holy Spirit', says John (Mark 1:8).

Those who did not admit their own sinfulness or their need of the Holy Spirit were the ones who were deaf to Jesus' message (Matthew 3:7-10). But the fact that so many ordinary people were willing to know themselves as sinners waiting for a saviour made it possible for Jesus' campaign to get off to a flying start (Mark 1:45).

The same goes for us, readers and hearers of Mark's Gospel. If we accept baptism, knowing and admitting we are sinners, then the way is open and straight for Jesus to give us his Spirit when we ask for it (Luke 11:13).

SEVENTY-ONE

Cloud of witnesses

Hebrews 12:1

The writer of Hebrews gives us a great cloud of witnesses and goes on to talk about persevering in the race that is set before us. The combination of these two images brings to mind the marathon race as it reaches the finish in the Olympic Games: the race started somewhere miles away, the contestants have managed to persevere so far, and now comes the climax, the finish. They enter the Olympic stadium and there find themselves surrounded by bank upon bank of seating filled with spectators. From the final running track it must feel like being cheered on by so many witnesses they look to reach the clouds.

The letter to the Hebrews is encouraging us to keep going to the end living a virtuous life. Keeping going is not easy, but it helps to know that the final quarter mile will be witnessed by a big crowd of supporters. That makes for a strong finish, even on weary legs. By this time the runners must often feel they are on their own, since the field has scattered and the runners are no longer in a bunch. When life becomes very difficult it helps to know that somebody cares, somebody is noticing. All along the way Jesus is our pacemaker, out in front but beckoning us to keep following.

In his letters, Paul the apostle also compares the life of a follower of Jesus to a race. We have to be careful with the way Paul says it: he reminds his readers that many compete in the big races, but there is only one winner. The reason we have to be careful is that in the life of a follower of Jesus competition plays no part: the good news has set us free from having to compete with one another. How does that come about?

The good news is that Jesus is the Son of God, and we are all his beloved sisters and brothers. We are all family, with our own reserved seat at our Father's table. Jesus our elder brother will not be satisfied as long as even one place at the table is still empty. The prize for the race we have run is a place at the table of God. We are all equally sons and daughters of God, and there is no higher honour, no higher privilege than that. Each of us is equally precious to God, since God is love and love has no favourites.

The honour that Jesus has won for us is beyond any honour or prize that human life has to offer. It is greater than that awarded to kings and queens, to athletes, to musicians or singers, to politicians or soldiers. Nobody can say, 'I am greater than you: get a life like mine, if you can!' My value depends on what God thinks of me, since God is truth.

Life is a race, though. What we are competing with is our own self: how to give God the very best life I am capable of. Life is meant to be about how we thank God for something we could not possibly earn or achieve, namely God's love. If we do well, that is only as it should be. If we do badly, there is still a consolation prize – God's love and forgiveness. And no one else can say, 'I came in ahead of you.'

SEVENTY-TWO

Brother, sister and mother

Mark 3:35

Mark tells us that one day Jesus had a crowd of listeners sitting around him (Mark 3:32). The crowd alerted Jesus to the fact that his mother and his brothers and sisters were 'outside', asking for him. They must have either been unable to draw close because of the crowd, or else they did not want to upset him by interrupting his teaching session. Then Jesus looked around at those who were sitting around him and said, 'Here are my mother and my brothers! Whoever does the will of God is my brother and sister and mother.'

As Christians we are well used to the idea of being brothers and sisters of Jesus. It is indeed part of the will of God that we should think of ourselves in this way. The good news of Jesus tells us that he himself is the Son of God and that we are his brothers and sisters, able and invited beyond all our deserving to call God '*Abba*! My Father,' as if we are little children learning from our elder brother. Christians down the ages have called one another 'brother' or 'sister' and tried to live out that family relationship both with Jesus and with one another around the world.

But what about our being the mother of Jesus? 'Whoever does the will of God is my mother', says Jesus, just as clearly as 'brother' or 'sister'. He is not saying, 'You women who do the will of God – you are my mother.' He is not saying 'My own mother Mary does the will of God, so she is doubly my mother.' That is true, but it is not only what Jesus is saying. No, anyone at all – man, woman or child – who does the will of God is mother to Jesus. So what does that mean?

Anyone who does the will of God is penetrated by the presence of God and becomes fruitful, bringing Jesus into the world alive and well in some other person or persons. It is an old saying that a good Christian is *alter Christus*, another Christ, bringing the love and forgiveness of Jesus where that love and forgiveness did not exist before. Everyone and anyone – man, woman or child – can become the mother of Jesus in some other person, once that person is inspired to hear what Jesus has to say to them. For myself, I can say with certainty that particular people in my life, including my own mother and father, have brought Jesus to life in me again and again in the course of my lifetime.

Why does Jesus not add, 'Whoever does the will of God is my father?' The reason is that although Jesus has many mothers, he has only one Father – the one in heaven. When Mark quotes Jesus as saying whoever leaves house or brothers or sisters or mother or father or children or fields for his sake will receive a hundredfold now in this age (Mark 10:29-30), he lists a hundredfold of houses, brothers, sisters, mothers, children and fields – but does not promise a hundredfold of fathers. Jesus has only one of those – the Father he shares with us. God can make any human being fruitful, bringing Christ to birth, but there is no way we can penetrate God and make God fruitful. Nobody brings the Father to birth.

But what an enormous privilege it is to bring Jesus to birth in another person!

SEVENTY-THREE

Two kinds of desolation

Mark 4:35-41

Desolation and consolation are two opposites often referred to by writers on spiritual things. Consolation is what we hope for from God – a feeling or a state of being in the right place, doing what God wants of us, at the right time. Even in times of sorrow or persecution, consolation can be there, deep down. Desolation, on the other hand, is a feeling or a state of being in the wrong place, doing the wrong thing, and not being able to see a way out of it.

We often talk in a non-scientific way about being in depression. Usually it means being down in the dumps, going nowhere in life, being in the grip of sadness. The sadness can be over something that has happened – perhaps a bereavement or being made redundant – or it can be for no apparent reason at all. There just doesn't seem to be any very good reason for getting out of bed in the morning.

The point I would like to make is this: we can equally feel depressed when we are over-stressed, too busy, too burdened; but the way to deal with that kind of depression is the exact opposite to the way to deal with the above 'glum' depression. To reach a state or a feeling of peace, the over-stressed kind needs a purposeful pruning of our activities. Sadly, we often think, 'Oh, I am depressed. I must work harder; I must shake off this depression,' which will just make the situation worse than ever.

In the Gospel stories, think about Martha making Jesus welcome in her home (Luke 10:38-42). The great artist Rembrandt has a drawing of Martha looking cross, pointing at her sister Mary just sitting there while she, Martha, is having to do all the work – kitchen tools hanging at her belt, chicken in a pot behind her. Jesus tells her to calm down, just to do the necessary, like Mary. Now, we might have said that Martha was depressed – she might have said the same of herself – but 'depression' seems to call for greater activity whereas Jesus wanted less activity.

This is why 'desolation' is probably a safer word to use in matters spiritual, rather than 'depression'. It is safer to limit the use of 'depression' when describing the state of sadness and being in need of cheering up. 'Desolation' is a less common word, but one that covers both ends of the scale. There are two kinds of desolation: the desolation of emptiness and the desolation of over-stress. Ignatius of Loyola, the author of the famous *Spiritual Exercises*, tells the spiritual guide to be aware of these two kinds of desolation: the state of mind and heart of the one being guided may need coaxing up or may need easing down. If the state of mind is not clear, he suggests to try easing down first, because a person of good will is more likely to overdo things out of generosity.

We seem to have come a long way away from the storm on the lake, our Gospel for today. But Jesus asleep there, his head on the helmsman's cushion, is an object lesson in stillness. He not only stills the storm, but he is also very still himself. The disciples are over-anxious about the storm, but they and the storm give us a clear picture of stress-type desolation, whereas Jesus shows us the peace and stillness to head for.

SEVENTY-FOUR

Left hand, right hand

Jonah 4:11

'And should I not be concerned about Nineveh, that great city, in which there are more than a hundred and twenty thousand people who do not know their right hand from their left?' That question, in which the prophet Jonah talks about the compassion of God, is surely one of the gentlest quotations in the whole of the Old Testament.

Jonah was instructed by God to go to Nineveh and threaten them with destruction if they did not mend their ways. The prophet was reluctant, and he sailed away in the opposite direction from where he was supposed to go. A storm later, and three days on the inside of a big fish, and Jonah finally went where he had been told to go. Nineveh was a great city – it took three days to walk across – and Jonah went through it telling everyone to repent if they wanted to avoid destruction. To his surprise, they all complied with God's wishes, from the king down to the least of the people and the animals(!). They took no food and no drink; they covered themselves with sackcloth and cried mightily to God for forgiveness. To Jonah's even greater surprise, God changed his mind about the calamity he had said he was going to bring down on them.

Jonah was cross as well as surprised: he had been expecting a starring role in the drama of the calamity. Then God spoke these wonderful words about 120,000 people who did not know their right hand from their left, and that is why he decided to have pity on them. The sentence conjures up a picture of God looking down on the whole world with pity for our confused minds and our mixed motives.

Right hand, left hand? Most of us are right handed, and we are quite skilled with our right hand; with our left hand we are clumsy. Thanks to our right hand, we think we can achieve wonders, whereas our left hand brings us back to reality. With our right hand we are ambitious, but our left hand can leave us feeling that we are a failure. (Our feet work the other way: for a right-handed person the left foot is the one that leads: 'Left, right, left, right!' You never hear soldiers going, 'Right, left, right, left!') For left-handed people, there is still the mixture of skill and clumsiness; it is simply the other way round: for them, the left hand is skilful; the right hand is a drawback. People who are ambidextrous are rare. Perhaps they are balanced; perhaps they do not need to know their right hand from their left.

These words attributed by Jonah to God are as comforting as any in the books of the Prophets. But even these are less comforting than the words of Jesus. In the Book of Jonah, it is because the citizens of Nineveh repented that God spared them, as well as the fact that they were mixed-up people. For Jesus, forgiveness comes first; repentance afterwards. Forgiveness comes first because each of us is a child of God, beloved daughter or beloved son. We do not know our right hand from our left because, like children in a cradle, we are still learning.

SEVENTY-FIVE

Own place at the table

Mark 7:27

The sacrament of baptism is one of the sacraments initiated by Jesus which confers a 'character', according to traditional theology. The sacrament confers a status which is lifelong, such that a person will never need to be baptised again, because the status can never be lost. The baptised one has a particular relationship with God the Father – God is father to this child – and from then on the relationship will never be lost. We cannot break it, and God will not break it.

Another traditional way of expressing the new status is to say that the one baptised has his or her own place at God's table, which no one else may take. If ever the baptised person strays from the family, the place is kept until the prodigal returns. In the meantime, Jesus the elder brother goes out in search of the stray. All other brothers and sisters are aware of the empty place, and they will do what they can to bring the missing sibling back to the family table.

There is a story in the Gospels that illustrates what it means to belong at God's table. Jesus is away in the region of Tyre, wanting to be unnoticed, when a woman who is a Gentile, of Syro-Phoenician origin, has heard about him and comes to him, persisting, wanting Jesus to cure her little daughter. The disciples with Jesus want him to send her away because she is so bothersome. Jesus seems to be willing at first, but for the fact that she is a Gentile; his mission from his Father is to see that the children of the family are fed – not, as he strangely puts it, to feed the family's dogs.

The woman by this time is bowing down at Jesus' feet. Taking up Jesus' image, she asks, as if she were a house dog under the table, for a crumb, a crumb of comfort from the table. In response, Jesus gives her exactly what she begged for in the first place, namely the cure of her daughter. In effect, Jesus has elevated a Gentile woman to the status of one of the children at the table because of her faith, and this story is one of those remembered by the apostles when they found themselves admitting Gentiles to baptism in the early Church. To all intents and purposes, Jesus has baptised this woman and given her a place at the table. Her little daughter, meanwhile, is free from her demon and lying on her bed, which rather sounds as if the demon was a restless and hyperactive demon.

This image of baptism as giving a place at the table is a very comforting one. It means that if ever we stray from God, our place is still there waiting for us, as the place of the prodigal son was still waiting for him (Luke 15:11-32). We have not lost it, and nobody else is allowed to take it. It also means that Jesus as Shepherd is out there searching for us, and when he finds us, that will be a matter of rejoicing.

SEVENTY-SIX

Stone upon stone

Mark 13:2

Jesus is sometimes compared to a cornerstone – the angled stone that slots into place between two walls and keeps them standing firmly together: Jew and Gentile, male and female, slave and free. At other times Jesus is compared to another key stone in a building: the foundation stone, upon which the whole building stands firm. I want to think for a while about the foundation stone.

Imagine a stonemason building a stone wall. First, the foundation is laid. Usually the foundation layer is not just one stone but a sequence of stones outlining the whole length of the wall or the building to be built. Then comes another layer of stones, all the way around and from end to end. Imagine if you were one of that layer of stones: you would be grateful for the strength below, without which you would not be able to stand tall.

Then picture another layer of stones being placed and fixed upon your layer. Usually the new stones are placed not directly upon another stone but between two lower-level stones, so as to share the weight.

As Jesus is coming out of the temple one day, one of his disciples marvels to Jesus about the size of the buildings and the size of the stones. Jesus is not over-impressed. He says, 'Do you see these great buildings? Not one stone will be left here upon another; all will be thrown down.' Peter, Andrew, James and John are among those who hear Jesus say this, and they ask him, when will this be?

After the resurrection we find Peter writing in his first letter, 'Come to him, a living stone, though rejected by mortals yet chosen and precious in God's sight, and like living stones, let yourselves be built into a spiritual house' (1 Peter 2:4-5). The physical temple was destined to come down, stone by stone. The temple built on the living stone which is Jesus is built up, stone upon stone.

Always Jesus is the foundation. Each generation after him rests ultimately on him, but we all help to carry the weight of the next generation, the next layer, as it is built on top of us: the weight of children is the most universal weight to be felt. Because of the love parents have for their children, the weight of responsibility is not felt as a burden – or at least, the burden is light. Each generation has the joy of being the top layer of the living wall for a time, until the builder comes round again and they find themselves with a family to care for.

The Gospel of John tells us about Jesus saying, prophesying about his own body, 'Destroy this temple, and in three days I will raise it up' (John 2:19). His death and resurrection will transfer the temple of God's presence from the doomed temple in Jerusalem to a living temple in which each of us is a living stone. Our foundation stone Jesus and the previous generations of Christians enable us to support our siblings and to care for our children.

SEVENTY-SEVEN

Water and fire

1 Kings 18:20-40

This story of Elijah challenging the 450 priests of Baal and defeating them may be a little hard to believe, but the message it gives is still very real and alive today, thousands of years later. To summarise the story, Elijah wanted to win back to God the people of the 12 tribes of Israel who were being seduced by the cult of the god Baal. He set up a competition: two bulls for sacrifice and two altars – one each for himself and the pagan priests. The bulls were killed and the offerings placed on the two altars, then it was up to the priests to call down fire on the wooden altar simply by praying to their god to set it alight. Elijah for his part would do the same, calling on the Lord, the God of Israel, to set fire to the altar simply in answer to his prayer.

The 450 prayed and pranced and danced all through the morning, and nothing happened to the offering of their bull. They carried on, gashing themselves till their blood ran, but still nothing happened as a result of their prayers. Then Elijah repaired the altar of the Lord, which had been thrown down. He put on 12 stones for the 12 tribes of Jacob, dug a trench all around the altar, cut the bull in pieces and laid them on the altar. Then, most remarkably, he called for 12 jars of water to be splashed over the offering – big jars, such that the water spilled over and filled the trench as well. Then he prayed to the Lord God of Abraham, Isaac and Jacob, and fire broke out that consumed the offering, the stones, the wood, the dust, and even the water.

Water first, and then fire. Is there a message in the story for today, one that may make clearer something that Jesus has left us in Christian worship? I think there is. When we are initiated as Christians, we are baptised with water. Either water is poured on our heads or else the candidate is totally immersed in water. The water stands for many things: for crossing the Red Sea from slavery to freedom, for crossing the River Jordan to enter the promised land, for cleansing, for slaking thirst, for calming deep anxieties, for total forgiveness.

Then, being so suddenly and completely set free as we are, sooner or later a fire is lit in our hearts. There comes a strong desire to thank God, to tell the world what has happened, and to share the gift that has been given. What comes to mind is the fire of Pentecost, when the Spirit promised by Jesus came down on the disciples where they were gathered in the one place: divided tongues, as of fire, came, and a tongue of fire rested on each of them (Acts 2:1-4). This was fire to warm their hearts, fire to convince them of the truths Jesus had taught them, and tongues of eloquence along with the desire to reach every language and race in the whole world.

Water first, then fire. The way Jesus always works: forgiveness first, then, once forgiven, a warmed heart to share the gift with the whole world.

SEVENTY-EIGHT

The Holy Spirit will come

Luke 1:35

The angel Gabriel was asked by Mary how she would come to have a child, as she was a virgin. The angel said to her, 'The Holy Spirit will come upon you, and the power of the Most High will overshadow you; therefore the child to be born will be holy; he will be called Son of God.' Why, we may wonder, was the Holy Spirit to come upon Mary at the same time as the conception of Jesus in her womb?

Perhaps the answer is to be found in something the apostle Paul tells us in his letter to the Romans and also in his letter to the Galatians. We, and the Romans, are told:

> All who are led by the Spirit of God are children of God. For you did not receive a spirit of slavery to fall back into fear, but you have received a spirit of adoption. When we cry, 'Abba! Father!' it is that very Spirit bearing witness with our spirit that we are children of God.
>
> *Romans 8:14-16*

To the Galatians, and to us his readers, Paul says much the same:

> Because you are children, God has sent the Spirit of his Son into our hearts, crying, 'Abba! Father!' So you are no longer a slave but a child, and if a child then also an heir through God.
>
> *Galatians 4:6-7*

So that seems to give the answer to why the Holy Spirit had a crucial role in the conception of Jesus. From the first moment of conception and ever afterwards he would have the same kind of relationship with God as any little child would have with his or her daddy. When he learns to speak and to pray as a little boy, Jesus instinctively uses the word *Abba* when speaking to God. His Father is God the Father. Jesus was the first in human history to dare to call God *Abba*, but with Jesus it is not daring; it is what comes from his very conception in Mary's womb.

Noticeably, Jesus still uses the word *Abba* when he is an adult, as if there is still a need to be like a little child if we hope to enter the kingdom. One could also wonder, what is the word used by the Son in addressing the Father from all eternity? Surely, the word would still be a heavenly version of *Abba*.

The first words spoken by Jesus in the Gospels occur after Mary and Joseph track him down to the temple when he is 12 years old. 'Why were you searching for me? Did you not know that I must be in my Father's house?' (Luke 2:49). Luke here does not use the word *Abba*, but he is translating that same word from Jesus' Aramaic into Greek; the giveaway is that Jesus is saying 'my Father', 'my Father's house', not 'God's house', or 'the dwelling place of the Lord.'

We can be endlessly grateful to Mark's Gospel for giving us the actual words spoken by Jesus during the agony in Gethsemane: 'Abba, Father, for you all things are possible; remove this cup from me' (Mark 14:36). Jesus speaks to God as a first-generation child of God, and he teaches us to do the same. By ourselves we would never dare to do that.

SEVENTY-NINE

Calling people names

Matthew 5:21, 22

This passage is part of Matthew's account of Jesus' Sermon on the Mount. 'You have heard that it was said to those of ancient times, "You shall not murder"; and "whoever murders shall be liable to judgement."' Then Jesus goes on to internalise the same commandment, bringing judgement to apply to bitter anger in the heart, out of which comes calling people names.

It seems that Jesus is depicting three degrees of anger. First comes simply being angry with a brother or sister; then comes using insulting words; thirdly comes calling a brother or sister 'You fool' and asking for them to be excluded from the community. Behind the words of Jesus here lies a new thought: whatever name I call someone else, that name in fact belongs to me rather than to the person I wish to insult. For the consequences Jesus promises the speaker are the very ones the speaker of insults wishes on the other, not realising the boomerang effect. If I call you a fool, then I am the fool for calling you one.

Jesus is not so much threatening his listeners with punishment from God as saying what the consequences are of being angry with others. 'Continue to do this, and that will follow.' What Jesus says about anger here follows a similar pattern to what he says about forgiveness in the same sermon: forgive others, and you will be free; judge others, and you will be tied up, in prison and in darkness (Matthew 6:14, 15). That is simply the consequence of failing to forgive. That is simply the nature of human relationships, from which we can learn if our hearts are open.

Some simple examples about anger are not hard to find. I judge a brother or sister to be a greedy person; yet this can often mean I am angry and irritated because the other has taken the best share of the cake without offering it to me first. In other words, I am the greedy one. Another brother or sister is very popular – more popular than I am. If something in my heart wishes that I were the popular one and that the admiring crowd would switch to follow me instead, then I am the mean and thoughtless one.

At a very ordinary level, this warning from Jesus can be a check on our anger. So, for instance, I find myself in my heart calling someone else lazy. Does that mean I am the lazy one who would dearly love to have nothing to do? Suppose I call someone else an idiot, in my heart or out loud. Does that mean I am the idiot for not recognising in the other a beloved son or daughter of God? In any encounter, it is far better to presume goodwill in the other person.

Lastly, what Jesus is saying here can be extended to calling oneself names. There is no profit in saying, 'You idiot' to myself about myself. If I am ready to acknowledge good gifts in another, those good gifts also apply to me.

EIGHTY

Precious

1 Peter 1:7, 18, 19

The first letter of Peter uses the word 'precious' twice, to talk about the genuineness of faith which is precious and imperishable even in the fire of persecution, and the precious blood of Christ which could provide a ransom infinitely better than silver or gold. We may wonder whether Peter, having been called 'Stone' by Jesus, liked to try out the imagery of precious stones – precious because they are imperishable. He had been forgiven for doing the worst thing he could have feared, so now he no longer fears his own weakness.

We are used to the imagery of sheep and shepherds as applied to the relationship between God and his people: Jesus as the Good Shepherd, ourselves as the sheep not just to remain as sheep but also called to assist in the shepherding of the flock. Likewise we easily remember Jesus calling four fishermen and promising that they would fish for people on his behalf. Is there not a useful image also behind the fact that Jesus called tax collectors? Not that Jesus saw his Way as some kind of tax: he makes clear to Peter on one occasion that the children of a king do not pay taxes, but they do make a voluntary contribution (Matthew 17:24-7).

Arguing with his enemies during Holy Week, Jesus holds up a coin of the realm, with the emperor's head impressed on it. 'Give therefore to the emperor the things that are the emperor's, and to God the things that are God's', says Jesus (Matthew 22:21). Surely the words of Jesus there invite us to see ourselves like coins with the image of God imprinted on us. From the beginning of creation we were made in the image of God; as with coins, the image upon us tells who we belong to and whose treasury vouches for us. If, then, we think about the apostolic side of this imagery, the task of the money collector is to gather the people with God's image upon them into God's treasury, away from thieves who have stolen them.

Like so many coins of gold, silver and copper, God's coins may become tarnished or covered with grime. The apostle will attempt to clear away the grime from the poor people who no longer know their own worth, to show them that they are precious to God and that underneath they are still God's beloved children.

Judas was paid 30 pieces of silver. That was how much Jesus' life and his blood were reckoned to be worth. Judas was cross at the waste of the precious ointment by the woman at the supper in Bethany (John 12:4). Three hundred denarii was too much to waste on Jesus! Poor Judas probably did not know what he was saying, possessed as he was with his love of money.

By contrast, then, the blood and the life of Jesus are precious and imperishable. They were not so jealously guarded by Jesus that he could not shed them rather than leave the human race in ignorance. God has forgiven our sins, no matter what anyone else says. In the fire of suffering, the message of Jesus is finally seen as truth.

EIGHTY-ONE

'Where you go, I will go'

Ruth 1:16, 17

This little song sung by Ruth to her mother-in-law Naomi is a useful one for a Christian to sing to Jesus. 'Where you go, I will go; where you lodge, I will lodge; your people shall be my people, and your God, my God.' In other words, 'your Father shall be my Father.' The song says finally, 'Heaven forbid that even death should part me from you', or words to that effect.

Jesus was a pilgrim all his life, and life for a Christian is a pilgrimage in the company of Jesus. It brings both the joys and the sorrows of being a pilgrim, and the need to be ready to let go at very short notice of the security of ownership because the Way of Jesus is calling me away.

Jesus was a carpenter, with his own carpenter's shop and business, presumably handed down by Joseph. For all of Jesus' teen years and through his twenties, Jesus was standing by, ready to leave it all behind when his Father called. According to the prophecies about God's Servant, he was like a sharpened sword waiting in its scabbard or like a polished arrow hidden in the quiver (Isaiah 49:2). The sign for Jesus to leave home came when John the Baptist began his work down by the River Jordan. Then Jesus shut up shop and probably left a notice on the closed door of the workshop, telling disappointed customers where the nearest carpenter's shop would be open! From then on, Jesus had nowhere to lay his head.

The same pattern applies across the whole of the human race, to some extent. Sooner or later, children normally leave home and make their own way, even though they have the support of their parents at a distance. The same happens in nature: take the example of the Great Crested Grebe, a diver bird that breeds on English lakes. The mother bird has a quaint way of encouraging her chicks to swim: she takes them for free rides over the water sitting on her broad back. Then one day she suddenly dives and leaves the chicks bobbing on the water. That kind of a day has to come for humans also, till we learn to cope on our own and to take responsibility for others.

I remember a little song that was written and sung by a young Danish girl. It tells of the joys of having no possessions, surprisingly enough. She was leaving home to go to university, so all home comforts were suddenly very dear; but if she wanted to find her own way in life, there was no point in letting the possessions possess her. They had to go.[13] The same girl was also a singer and performer of her own songs, and that also calls for flexibility: to be able to entertain, to love and be loved by audience after audience, but then to move on and sing somewhere else, like a troubadour.

The most unusual thing about this songstress was that she enjoyed going on pilgrimages, walking cross-country to holy shrines with like-minded companions. This helped to make sense of the pilgrimage of daily life: no point in taking the kitchen sink with you if you are going on foot to somewhere else.

---

13. 'No Possessions' written and performed by Lea Bostrop Renne. From the album *Road* by Laybann, 2013.

EIGHTY-TWO

Not far

Mark 12:28-34

This discussion between one of the scribes and Jesus takes place in the context of the week we call Holy Week. He asks Jesus to reckon which commandment is the greatest of all. Clearly what the scribe means is, which commandment of the Law – the Law of Moses – is the greatest of them all. The Gospel of Matthew in referring to the same incident makes that clear (Matthew 22:36). Here in Mark's Gospel it is Jesus who provides the answer, and then the scribe agrees with him: the first is to love the Lord our God 'with all your heart, and with all your soul, and with all your mind, and with all your strength'.

The second, for Jesus, is, 'You shall love your neighbour as yourself.' Again the scribe agrees with Jesus. Indeed, in Luke's Gospel it is the scribe himself who comes up first with the same answer (Luke 10:26-8). Then, here in Mark's version of the story, Jesus congratulates the scribe and tells him, 'You are not far from the kingdom of God.' Notice that Jesus does not tell the scribe, 'You have reached the kingdom of God', but rather that he is on the way and has not far to go.

For some reason, teachers often speak about these two commandments as if they were Jesus' own two great commandments, whereas they had actually been there for centuries. If the commandments of the old Law were the only things Jesus came to tell us, why would he have to die on a cross at the instigation of the scribes and Pharisees?

Jesus' new commandment is that we should love one another as he loved us – and not just friends, brothers and sisters, but enemies too. As he loved us . . . That is different from the first command of the old Law. Jesus is saying, look at how I and my Father have loved you, and then, in gratitude for our unconditional love, learn to love one another. The old Law as it is written looks as if it is ordering us to love God, and you cannot really order anyone to love.

The old Law uses the expression, 'Love your neighbour as yourself' only once, in a place where it means 'Love your Jewish neighbour as yourself' (Leviticus 19:18). Jesus updates that to mean we must love our enemies as well, as in his story of the good Samaritan (Luke 10:29-37). The other commandments of the Decalogue – the Ten

Commandments of Moses – Jesus does not leave standing as they are; in the Sermon on the Mount (Matthew 5–7) he internalises some of them so that scribes and lawyers cannot turn them into dead letters.

Jesus seems to have detected goodwill in the scribe who asked the question. That in itself would have brought the scribe closer to the kingdom of God. To have asked this dangerous teacher Jesus a genuine question, and then to agree with his reckoning as regards the greatest commandment, took courage. And it is quite marvellous that between them, Jesus and the scribe came up with the same brief sentence for second choice: 'Love your neighbour as yourself' – a sentence that was only written once in the whole of the Old Testament.

EIGHTY-THREE

When you give a banquet

Luke 14:12-14

This passage in Luke's Gospel, about who to invite when you are throwing a party, has been listened to by people of goodwill more often than some other sayings of Jesus. There are facilities available to the poor, the crippled, the lame and the blind in more cities and towns than was the case in Jesus' time. Obviously there is a long way to go, but in one person's lifetime there have been the Paralympics (on a grand scale) and wonderful establishments such as the Leonard Cheshire Homes and the Sue Ryder Homes, where people with physical disabilities are enabled to live as near normal lives as is possible. Even the poor have somewhere to go to obtain a meal in most big cities, and they meet there by courtesy of volunteer cooks. The implication is that the poor are not poor by nature, but are victims of circumstances which will change.

There is a broad principle at work in this short illustration from Jesus. To give to those who cannot pay you back is better than to give to friends, brothers, relatives or rich neighbours. These latter will sooner or later be generous to you in return, in which case the gift you gave was more like a deal than a real gift. To give without any hope of return is the real gift. Why? Because that is the way God gives.

The prime example of giving without hope of return is surely to be found in parents when they are looking after their infant children. Infants take it for granted that mother or father or both will come to the rescue in every possible need. The hour of the day or night is irrelevant – baby wants attention, and lets the want be known. Often it is only when those children become parents themselves that they realise how much it costs, and so their respect for their own parents increases enormously. 'Did you two do all this for me when I was tiny?!'

One result of Jesus' speaking to God as *Abba*! is that it alerts us to our own helplessness, like the helplessness of little children. God is very good to us, and yet it is not until we have to care for others that we realise just how good God is to us.

God is like a shepherd, and he has been caring for me his lamb from the moment of my conception. But it is not until I have become a shepherd of people myself that I realise the anxious care, hope, planning, sleepless nights and longing love that are part of a genuine carer's lot.

Not just carers but also teachers have to provide a 'banquet' for their pupils, and very often they receive little or no thanks for it at the time. Pupils who become teachers in time soon discover the thanklessness of much of the task. Christian clergy, too, are called upon to be a rock of strength for their people, while at the same time they often feel weak themselves.

God the First Person of the Trinity is the one who gives without conditions, even where no love comes back. Jesus our Lord is the one who does the same: he gives thanks to the Father, and then loves you and me with no conditions.

EIGHTY-FOUR

Your Father feeds them

Matthew 6:26

Some things we take for granted, things which in fact have come about in interesting and instructive ways. For example, as Christians of the twenty-first century of the Christian era we quite happily sing, quoting God in the Book of Isaiah, 'I will never forget you, my people. I have branded your name on the palm of my hand' (see Isaiah 49:15-16). Words like those were not originally spoken to today's Christians; they were for the people of Israel two and a half thousand years ago. How comes it that we confidently take these words to ourselves?

'Does a mother forget her baby at the breast, or does a woman forget the child within her womb? Even if they should forget, I will never forget you, city of Zion' (see Isaiah 49:15). We sing that one too, which the prophet addressed to the city of Zion 2500 years ago. How does it come about that we as Christians apply the prophet's words not just to all the faithful, but to each and every one of us? I sing a hymn like that and I am the one God will never forget, no matter what happens. The odds against a mother forgetting her baby are mighty, but the odds against God forgetting me are mightier yet: it will just never happen.

It is Jesus who makes the old songs personal to all his disciples, and who continues to do the same today. Jesus takes all the faithful love of God in the history of the Jews and gives it to each of his disciples, one at a time. God has not changed, but the gates are open to anyone with faith, to anyone who wants to believe.

Have you perhaps noticed that when Jesus is telling people not to be anxious and praises the trusting behaviour of the bird population, he says, 'They neither sow nor reap nor gather into barns, and yet your heavenly Father feeds them'? He does not say, 'Their heavenly Father feeds them,' because God is not their heavenly Father. God is Father to you and me, but not to the birds or the flowers of the field. God is the creator of nature and of human nature, but the family relationship is only with us, all unworthy though we are.

Add to that the way Jesus provides us with two versions of his 'Rabbi's prayer': the one we use most ('Our Father', Matthew 6:9-13) and the one we tend to forget ('My Father', Luke 11:2-4). All the love

God has for his people he has for you and for me, cherished members of his family.

We could also say we are close to the Father's heart, as John's Gospel says of Jesus (1:18). The beloved disciple is closest to the heart of Jesus at the Last Supper, and that is where every beloved disciple belongs – closest to Jesus who is closest to the Father's heart.

EIGHTY-FIVE

Be imitators of God

Ephesians 4:31–5:2

Let me say what I think 'imitating God' is all about. It involves taking into account the holy Trinity – three Persons, one God.

The Father, namely the First Person, is Love with no beginning or end, love with no conditions, love that does not depend on anyone else's love, love that nobody else loved into being, the live fire that nobody ever lit.

The Lord Jesus, now revealed as Son of God and the Second Person of the Trinity, is Love-in-return-for-love, who from all eternity received the love of the Father with thanks, praise and endless affection.

The Holy Spirit, the Third Person, is the messenger of love from Father to Son and back from Son to Father. Through the Holy Spirit, love is safely received and safely returned.

Where we humans come in, if we are to imitate God, is by aligning ourselves with Jesus. There is a magnetism of love going on always between the First and Second Persons, and we are invited, as it were, to step into the Trinity alongside Jesus. With Jesus for my brother, I receive the gifts and privileges of being a child of God without ever deserving such gifts. The Holy Spirit delivers to me the love of the Father. The first way of imitating God is to let the Father love me without my deserving love. Alongside Jesus I become a beloved child of God, a lamb of God.

The Second Person, our Jesus, urges us to do as he did and to love God back, to love in return for love. Like Jesus, we are called not simply to be passive and enjoy being loved, but also to praise, love and delight in the Father, and to do his will by drawing as many other humans as we can into the same circle of love. We are called to be not just a child, but also a willing servant, not just God's lamb but also God's shepherd, looking to gather in the lost sheep.

As apostles, servants or shepherds, we are invited to love as God loves – faithfully, whether or not love and affection are coming back. Unstoppable love will win through in the end. We do not so much need to pray for God's love for ourselves, since that is there for us all the time and all we have to do is believe in it. But the love that goes back in the other direction, although it is felt, is often beyond our power to create. Think how the disciples of Jesus believed in God's love shown to them by Jesus, but when it came to imitating his love under persecution they were found wanting; they should have prayed for strength. The Holy Spirit comes again to those who ask, to help us show to God the sort of love that has been shown to us first.

Notice, too, how the apostles and other disciples were not abandoned by Jesus when they let him down so badly. The love that comes towards us never fails, even if we fail in our efforts to pass it on.

EIGHTY-SIX

Places at table

Luke 14:7-11

Long ago there was a book of cartoon illustrations telling (tongue in cheek), *How to Be Topp*. The author, as far as I remember, was pretending to be a boy at a prep school and describing the best ways to achieve top honours without really trying. At first sight, Jesus in this passage from Luke seems to be doing the same. He describes how to make it to the top table at a wedding banquet without apparently trying. Go for the top and you may lose it; go for the lowest place and you stand a good chance of being promoted to the top table. Is Jesus simply advising us on the best way to make it to the top? Does that not give a strange picture of humility, namely not humble at all?

This passage in Luke needs to be taken alongside other sayings of Jesus about merit, or rather poverty of merit. Jesus usually tells us not to count our merits, because if we tot them up and find ourselves rather superior to other people, then we are suffering from pride, whereas if we find ourselves short of merits then we are liable to suffer from depression. Best of all is to do our best always but not keep score.

When you think about it, to ask God to reward us according to our merits is a rash and foolish prayer. A life of virtue and thought for others receives a medal from the Queen, and that is the end of it. Who wants to get to heaven, be given a medal and then be pushed into a corner: 'You have had your reward!' To leave ourselves open to God, aware that we deserve nothing, is the best and the wisest way. Every good thing we have ever done is a gift from God, so ultimately each of us is a beggar, although some have had more than their share of donations dropped into their begging bowl.

So, to get back to Jesus' parable about places at the wedding banquet, if I go for the top table, I am thinking about my merits and looking for reward here and now. That is pride. If I go to the bottom place and sit down, I am agreeing that I am a beggar in the sight of God, deserving of nothing and relying on God's generosity and forgiveness for letting me have a place at all. God is never outdone in generosity, and there has to be more to heaven than medals.

Places at table

One of the most beautiful things about Christian baptism is that it gives the baptised one a place at the table: not the best place, not the lowest place, but a fixed place. Nobody else can have it. I am this beloved daughter of God or this beloved son of God, and each time God looks for me, he knows where to look along the table. Every place at the wedding table has a name written there ('Your names are written in heaven,' says Jesus in Luke 10:20, and this is where they are written). Nobody else may have your place, nor you theirs. Much the best to sit down at the lowest place and let your host direct you to the place that is yours, and yours alone.

EIGHTY-SEVEN

When the Spirit of truth comes

John 16:12-15

I would like to suggest a few unusual images to help us to picture what the Holy Spirit does for us and is for us, and to suggest how the Spirit relates to the Father and the Son and reaches into the depths of each.

The first image is homesickness. Imagine you are praying about the Way of the Cross, using your imagination to picture Jesus carrying his cross on the way to Golgotha. Along the way, Jesus is so weak that the soldiers feel he may never reach the place of execution, so they compel a passer-by, who was coming in from the country, to carry his cross; it was Simon of Cyrene. Here we have in picture form the Way of Jesus that his disciples follow: Jesus and I are yoked together, he carrying my cross and I carrying his. We are journeying along the Way.

Jesus then, as always, is going home to his Father in heaven. That is what he has been doing all his life, but now the time is closer. I, yoked to Jesus, have been invited to see the Father of Jesus as my Father also. Where Jesus will be at home, there also will I be at home. I am an orphan no longer.

The Father of Jesus calls me from the far side of the cross. The homesickness in my heart speaks the presence of the Holy Spirit, who proceeds from the Father. The homesickness proceeds also from Jesus, my companion on the Way. He longs to be home in heaven, having completed the task he was given. Homesickness in God is a two-way longing: home longing for me and me longing for home.

Stories Jesus told often included images of home, of belonging. The most famous of all, the story of the prodigal son (Luke 15:11-32), has a very clear picture of a father longing for his wayward son to come back. The father's yearning, with his eyes fixed on the road his son might come down, is overwhelming. The son who comes back has a rather self-centred reason for coming back, but the welcome home is wholehearted. The parable of the lost sheep gives us a homesickness that is more evenly matched: the shepherd searches high and low for the lost one; the lost one is not enjoying being lost, and is probably as glad to be found as the shepherd is to find it and carry it home (Luke 15:3-7).

Children in boarding schools usually feel homesick at first, longing for home as home equally misses them. People in prison are the same: longing and longed for. At a deep level, we all come from God, and our hearts are restless until we go back there.

Here is another useful image to depict the Holy Spirit: take two magnets of the traditional horseshoe shape and snap them together. Let one be the First Person and the other the Second Person; the magnetism invisibly circling through both magnets is like the Holy Spirit. What is more, if we place a small piece of metal such as a paper clip to the side of one magnet, the magnetism flows through that as well. Thus, if we cling to Jesus, his homesickness flows through us as well.

EIGHTY-EIGHT

Wings like eagles

Isaiah 40:28-31

Isaiah tells us that God does not faint or grow weary. There is a lovely image somewhere from the early Christian writers that says that the light of love and forgiveness is always shining from God, and all the sinner has to do is to turn round and come face to face with God who never stopped loving. We sinners run away from God, so all we can see is our own shadow stretched out in front of us. The further we run, the longer the shadow, so we think, 'I can never turn round now; I have gone too far; I can never retrace my steps.' But, said this ancient Christian writer, we have only to turn round where we are to see the smile of welcome that never left the face of God. Then we can start trying again to live a better life and to move back towards the light of God's love.

Isaiah also says, in today's Bible passage:

Even youths will faint and be weary, and the young will fall exhausted; but those who wait for the Lord will renew their strength, they shall mount up with wings like eagles, they shall run and not be weary, they shall walk and not faint.

Where does the power come from? 'He gives power to the faint, and strengthens the powerless.' God's constant love and forgiveness is what gives us the strength to continue even when we feel we have failed.

Little birds like finches fly with tiny bursts of energy. They rest between each flutter of wings and do not fly very far before they have to stop and rest. Not so the eagles: once off the ground they seem to be effortless; they swoop and soar with hardly a flap of their huge wings; distance is no problem; storms no trouble. Birdwatchers nowadays tell us the eagles are not alone: humble swifts apparently leave the nest and fly for a whole year, then they touch down to build their own nests the following spring. They even sleep on the wing!

But eagles are the best models. Rather than be upset and paralysed because we have been at fault somewhere, we listen to Jesus saying, 'Son, your sins are forgiven; daughter, your sins are forgiven. Don't freeze; just carry on, trying to do your best. God never changes, so neither need you change. Distance is no problem; storms no trouble.'

It occurs to me that although God has forgiven me, there may be people I have hurt who have definitely not forgiven me. Put it this way: Jesus has let me come into his kingdom as a forgiven sinner. If those who have not forgiven me want to enter the kingdom, they will have to learn to forgive me. Jesus will not expel me at the behest of anyone else. Jesus believes in the forgiveness of sins.

The chapter of Isaiah we started with today includes a reference that is especially pleasing to mothers and school teachers. After a line about God gathering the lambs in his arms, Isaiah adds that God will 'gently lead the mother sheep' (verse 11). Mothers have eagles' wings as well.

EIGHTY-NINE

Gift and invitation

John 15:12

Jesus in the Gospels is often repeating the same message but using different images – for instance, sheep and shepherds. As a sheer gift, we are all sheep and lambs of God's flock, and that is guaranteed. After that, we are invited to become shepherds ourselves and to care for our own flock with the same care and dedication that Jesus has shown us. If we succeed, well and good; if we fall down on the job, that does not stop the divine shepherd from loving us. In fact, when Jesus said his disciples would do even greater things than he himself had done, this may be one of them: Jesus never had to blame himself for moral failure and then carry on trying. The rest of us frequently have to swallow our pride and start again.

Think of the image of light and warmth. God's love shown to us in Jesus is guaranteed, and all we have to do is believe in it. Then we are invited to share that light with one another, if possible with great faithfulness and dedication to the needs of one another. Again, if we succeed, well and good; if we fail, God's love for us is still the same, and we are invited to have another try.

We are God's children, beloved sons and daughters. That never ceases to be true, even when we fail to behave like children of our God and king. God does not love us for our good works and then disown us when we fall down; God loves us because we are his children, the way any good parents love their children.

Jesus is the Way, and he teaches us how to find the Way to eternal life. I do not have to pay for lessons, as learner drivers of cars have to: Jesus instructs me for free. Then I am invited to share my knowledge of the Way with others, whether it be children, the poor, the slow learners, the sick, the lonely, or whoever I encounter in my daily life. If I turn out to be good at sharing, well and good. If I am determined to be self-centred, Jesus still offers his Way to me – the way of humility: I am a forgiven sinner, so I can always try again, as Peter and the other disciples did once they had learned to pray for strength.

Jesus calls fishermen – Peter, Andrew, James and John. He, so to speak, nets them from aimlessly swimming around to be at home in his baptism. Then he turns them into fishers for people, who will net people into the life and ways of Jesus. Jesus does the same with us: he gathers us in, then without ever losing us he invites us to tempt others into the same way of life by letting the world see the beauty of it. He wants us to be not just contented Christians but happy people always looking to share our happiness.

Jesus calls a blind beggar. 'Take heart; get up, he is calling you,' the people in the crowd around Jesus say to Bartimaeus (Mark 10:49). Bartimaeus has been crying louder and louder to Jesus to please have pity on him. He wants to see again, and once he receives back his sight he follows Jesus on the Way. Jesus gives, and then the invitation is there to follow on the Way.

NINETY

To forgive or to retain?

John 20:21-3

According to John's Gospel, Jesus appears to the 11 chosen disciples on the evening of the day he rose again and says these words: 'Peace be with you. As the Father has sent me, so I send you.' Then he breathes on them and says to them, 'Receive the Holy Spirit. If you forgive the sins of any, they are forgiven them; if you retain the sins of any, they are retained.'

It seems to me unlikely that Jesus is giving the apostles freedom to put a block on the forgiveness of sins wherever they fancy: it seems more likely that they are being empowered to forgive whatever Jesus himself forgave, and to retain the sins that he retained, so as to keep alive the Way of Jesus now that his presence is with them in a different way from how things were before his death.

Jesus forgave unstintingly. He forgave tax collectors who squeezed money out of the poor and defenceless. He did not condemn the woman caught in the act of adultery. He forgave those who were murdering him. He forgave Peter for denying him out of fear of the soldiers who arrested Jesus and out of fear of the high priest's maidservant who threatened to give him away. He did not condemn Pilate for condemning him, but acknowledged Pilate's authority. He declared forgiven the paralysed man let down through the roof on a stretcher, without even enquiring what sins might be on the man's conscience. He told the woman who washed his feet with her tears that her sins were forgiven, to the astonishment of his Pharisee host at the meal.

What sins, then, did Jesus retain? I think they all relate to judging others and not forgiving others. Jesus believes in the forgiveness of sins, so those who will not forgive are putting themselves into the opposing camp. John the Baptist prepared the Way by encouraging people to acknowledge that they were sinners and that they were in need of forgiveness (Matthew 3:1, 2). The enemies of Jesus were those who thought they were not sinners and that everyone apart from themselves was a sinner. They thought they did not need forgiving, since they were already covered by the Law.

Jesus' sweeping statement, 'Do not judge, and you will not be judged' (Luke 6:37), has another side to it, namely, 'Judge, and you will be judged.' If we are self-righteous while we condemn other people, then the words of Jesus pull us up short. Surely the disciples to whom Jesus appears on that resurrection day are being commissioned to uphold his standard of forgiveness. The sin against the Holy Spirit (Luke 12:10) cannot be forgiven as long as we persist in it, but is readily forgiven if we admit we are sinners and learn to forgive everyone else, friend or foe.

For Jesus, forgiveness comes first, then he hopes that repentance follows. 'Zacchaeus, hurry and come down; for I must stay at your house today' (Luke 19:5). Jesus even called Judas, who betrayed him, 'Friend': 'Friend, why are you here?' (Matthew 26:50, RSV). Jesus was only at loggerheads with those who thought themselves perfect while they condemned all others. This, surely, is the Way the apostles and disciples are to follow, the sins they are to retain, until there is a change of heart.

NINETY-ONE

Treasure hidden in a field

Matthew 13:44

'The kingdom of heaven is like treasure hidden in a field, which someone found and hid; then in his joy he goes and sells all that he has and buys that field.'

We all enjoy news stories of searchers with metal detectors who unearth hidden hordes of treasure from a bygone age. These days the finder is not usually able to hide and keep the treasure because the field is not his, though he has the farmer's permission to search. Besides that, in our country, a treasure trove is the property of the Crown, though said Crown will usually give a generous percentage of the value of the find to the finder and the farmer.

In spite of the way a treasure trove is hedged with restrictions, this parable of Jesus still appeals to the romantic in us: if there is treasure to be found, yes, please, I would like to be the one to find it.

For some time now I have tended to equate the field in Jesus' story to the Christian Church. I picture a field 200 by 100 metres, extensive, filled with all sorts of earth, wild plants and rubbish. Taking my metal detector over the ground, I discover treasure, and in consequence I buy the whole field for the sake of the treasure. There are many things about the Church that are not helpful; there are some aspects of the Church that are positively harmful. But I still buy the field, the Church, because of the treasure I have found.

What did I find? Well, I found forgiveness, not only for the past but also for the future. What could be more precious than that? I found love from God and from fellow Christians, and a warm invitation to improve the lot of the world in company with like-minded Christians. Any number of things can go wrong within the Church, but hope is found there beyond any hope offered anywhere else in the world.

The treasure initially intrigues the searcher. It includes what at first looks just like a book, or a collection of books. Then when the searcher delves into the book he finds, or she finds, not shadows of the past but a vibrant, living Person, namely Jesus himself, still and again alive, loving and inviting.

Led by the words of the book, the searcher can find what God is saying day by day and moment by moment, bringing the gift of knowing myself to be in the right place at the right time and doing the right thing for God. Besides the words of the book there are ceremonies Jesus founded: these are not always presented as I would wish, but they are always a direct link to Jesus; they are what he wanted us to do in his memory.

There are so many wonders hidden within the treasure, I have never regretted buying the field. And I would never advise anyone else to give up on the field.

NINETY-TWO

A sword to guard the way

Genesis 3:24

The gates of Paradise were shut to humankind, 'and at the east of the garden of Eden [God] placed the cherubim, and a sword flaming and turning to guard the way to the tree of life.'

I want to muse for a minute or two: did God ever shut the gates of Paradise, or did we humans just presume they were shut after seeing our own sinfulness? Did Jesus not show us in his baptism that the heavens were split open, that there was no block between him and God? Was that a sudden decision on God's part or had the road always been open, only we could not see it was open? Did God change and suddenly become generous? Surely not! Surely God was always Love, only we could not see it; we were blind.

When Jesus died on the cross, the veil hiding the presence of God in the Holy of Holies was torn in two, from top to bottom. The death of Jesus was what it took, not to change God's mind but to open our eyes to the depth, strength and endurance of God's love for us.

There are different ways of wondering what was the original sin. For John Milton it had to be pride – the desire to be equal to God. For some others it was ingratitude: our first parents, according to the story in Genesis, had a paradise garden with everything they could ever need or want; yet they concentrated their greedy attention on the one and only tree they were told, for their own good, not to touch. When Jesus came he taught us gratitude: life for Jesus and then for his followers is acknowledgement of the endless gifts of God and then a constant attempt to show gratitude. For others the original sin would have to be lack of trust, not trusting that the one tree (in the story) was barred for our own good. Jesus then is seen as teaching us the trust of little children, able to call God *Abba* as he did himself.

The prophets of the Old Testament, one after another, promised reconciliation and peace from God. They introduced and reintroduced a covenant between God and the children of Abraham, a covenant that was conditional upon good behaviour but which was renewed each time in spite of the lack of good behaviour. Time and again the covenant was broken, but each time there was another prophet to announce God's willingness to try again. Prophets began to wonder if there would be a new covenant even more generous than the previous ones, but who would be the one to put it into words? Jesus was the one, with a covenant that could not be broken between God and every human child: God would love us not because we are good children, but because we are his children. Such a promise cannot be a sudden notion on God's part: this must have been the plan all along.

The poet Francis Thompson pictures God saying:

All which thy child's mistake
fancies as lost, I have stored for thee at home:
rise, clasp My hand, and come.[14]

---

14. Francis Thompson, 'The Hound of Heaven' in *The Poems of Francis Thompson*, London: Oxford University Press, 1937.

NINETY-THREE

Before the foundation

Ephesians 1:4, 5

Paul, writing to the Christians of Ephesus, says that God 'chose us in Christ before the foundation of the world . . . He destined us for adoption as his children through Jesus Christ . . .' If that is true about the church members at Ephesus at the time Paul visited and stayed some months with them, he must mean it to be true about all the Christians in all the churches he visited. And if it is truly said about them, then it can be truly said about any follower of Jesus who believes in him, anywhere, any time. How does it feel to know that God had me in mind for adoption before the foundation of the world?

If God was thinking about me before the universe was created, before the 'Big Bang' sent the stars spinning on their endless quest, surely he who knows every star by name will not forget me. I and you are at the forefront of God's purpose; we are not accidental. Each of us has our own name branded on the hand of God so that he will not forget. Each of us has our own place at his table, earmarked and kept safe until the day of our arrival.

What Paul says in that letter to the Ephesians could remind us of one of Jesus' own most amazing statements. We recall Jesus saying, 'Before Abraham was born, I am' (John 8:58). That was enough for the hostile crowd to pick up stones ready to kill him for blasphemy. Yet here is Paul saying something very similar about even the most insignificant of Jesus' followers. Each of us can say, 'Before Abraham was, I am there in Christ.'

Eternity is a mystery to us in our present state, but it seems to be rather regardless of time, and time before or time after. So, for instance, there is probably no need to think of a future judgement when I die and then a general judgement at the end of time. When I die, surely I will step out of time and into eternity, so how can there be an age of time before the end of the world? If I am no longer in time, then there will be no waiting time. When we die, that is the end of the world for each of us.

Really, eternity is now; eternity is with us. Jesus comes from a world that is not governed by time, a world where love and forgiveness is the rule, and he brings that world with him. The air is different in his world, and we have to learn to breathe love and forgiveness to stay in it. But his values are eternal – without beginning and without end: they always were true, before the foundation of the world, and they always will be true, beyond the end of time.

Even forgiveness is eternal, surely. It would not seem right to suggest that God only started forgiving when creatures started to be disobedient.

NINETY-FOUR

Wedding robe

Matthew 22:1-14

In Matthew's version of the wedding banquet story, the audience is invited to compare the kingdom of God to this banquet. Jesus is pointing out how over the centuries the people were invited to celebrate with God, but they did not listen to the message of the prophets. Instead they went their own ways, ignoring the fact that they were like common people turning down a generous invitation from royalty. Worse than that, they maltreated and killed the prophets – the messengers who were sent by God the king to invite them. In the story, the king was furious, sent his troops, destroyed the murderers and burnt their city.

Probably in the time of Jesus kings might well behave like that, but is Jesus saying that God would behave like that? There is certainly, for Jesus, a consequence to be expected if they do not listen to him, the latest of the prophets: their city, the city of Jerusalem, will be burnt down and destroyed. After that, all sorts of people will be invited, deserving or undeserving, good or bad, and they will receive the blessings that were originally meant for the first people invited.

The message for us readers and hearers of the gospel is to esteem our own invitation as Gentiles to the kingdom of God. This is something we never deserved; something so precious that only came to us because God's own people did not want it when the invitation came through Jesus. This is eternal life; this is the love of God, and we have been adopted as God's children.

What, then, of the man who went to the wedding banquet without a wedding robe? Why is he thrown out again to the darkness outside? We have all been invited, but how can we be sure that we have a wedding robe to put on? How do we manage to stay in the banquet?

These people in the story were bundled in to the banquet from off the streets – everyone they could find. Would they have been walking the streets with a wedding robe at hand, on the off-chance they might be invited to a wedding? In Luke's version of the story the guests are brought in not just from the streets of the town but also from the roads and lanes round about (Luke 14:21-23). It seems to me the only way each of such a motley crowd could have had a wedding robe is if the king provided a kaftan at the door for them to put on, at his expense.

What, then, of the one man without? He must have thought he was worthy enough without help from the king. In our case, if we think we are worthy of heaven and that we do not need to be forgiven, we are sadly mistaken. The wedding robe, I would say, is God's forgiveness, and we must be ready to wear it.

NINETY-FIVE

The hairs of your head

Matthew 10:30

Every now and then, Jesus comes up with a statement very different from the way the Old Testament speaks about God. For his ancestors, God seemed to be more concerned with the nation as a whole than with each small individual. The people went down into Egypt and were all put to slavery. They escaped along with Moses, evidently not leaving any of their number behind, but in the desert many of them perished. Many more died in the struggle to find a home in the Promised Land, then more in the further battles trying to hang on to the new homeland.

When most of the dwellers in the land were taken into exile in Babylon, the concern was that the nation should not be wiped out. A remnant had to come back and start again, and rebuild the temple in Jerusalem. Even when the land was subjected to the Roman conquerors, they tried valiantly to preserve their identity as a people, a people out of whom the Messiah would one day come.

The Messiah comes in the form of Jesus, and he is unusually concerned with people one by one, especially those who are usually left in the margins: the blind, the lame, the deaf, the sick. For Jesus, God is *Abba*, a personal, first-generation Father, and not just a creator or remote ancestor. The rest of us are invited to see ourselves as family – his brothers and sisters – and to celebrate this as a gift from God.

The verse we heard just now, about the hairs of our head all being counted, is just one example of the incredibly close relationship between God and each one of us, as described by Jesus. None of us could count the hairs on our head; even those given to the current men's fashion of shaving the head bald could not tell you the number of roots that will start again if allowed. Even for someone afflicted with an ailment that kills off all hairs, there is the fact that God knows every breath that we breathe, every beat of our heart, and (according to Psalm 56:8) has collected in a bottle every tear we ever shed.

An exercise worth doing is to think how God not only gazes at me from out there somewhere, but that God is within me, looking out through my eyes and seeing exactly what I see. If I am in the good habit of talking to God about what I am seeing and experiencing, I am in fact presuming that God sees exactly what I see from my angle: I do not have to set the scene so that God will know what I am talking about. If there are dozens of us in the same room, we each have our own angle on what we see, and none of us could see a thing unless God and life was underpinning our vision.

What Jesus says about the hairs of our head is for him almost a throwaway line, something he sees as so obvious that it hardly needs saying. But if we take it to heart, what a wonderful closeness to God is there: God who is love looking out with me through my eyes; God who is not so preoccupied with the stars that he would overlook any one of us. And now that Jesus is risen and ascended to the Father, we can make a daily friend of Jesus if we so wish, sharing what we see and what we feel with someone who is both loving and deeply interested.

NINETY-SIX

They also serve

Psalm 123

The psalm today gives an unusual picture of service. We normally think of service as meaning doing things, keeping busy. But here in the psalm we have a picture of a king and a queen – or at any rate a master and a mistress – seated and holding court. Before them are standing the manservants and the maidservants, as yet doing nothing. Then the master gives a look or beckons in the direction of one of the manservants, because he has a job for him to do. Then, too, the queen or the mistress looks at or beckons to one of the maidservants, to indicate that there is a task for her.

Until the call comes or a finger of the hand beckons, the servants are servants, but they are only waiting. As the poet John Milton wrote about his own blindness, 'They also serve who only stand and wait.'[15]

We can become restless and uncomfortable before God, wondering if what we are doing with our lives is what God really wants of us. There is a feeling that goes with low moods whereby we constantly wonder if we really should be somewhere else, doing something different. At such times the Psalm 123 idea is very useful: 'I am here, Lord, doing what seems to be best. If you want me to be doing something else, somewhere else, please let me know; give me a clear signal. But in the meantime I hope to do wholeheartedly what I am already doing for you.'

This can become a more extended prayer:

> Take my eyes, Lord God, and if there is anything or anyone you want me to see, then direct my eyes there.
>
> Take my ears, that I might hear if I am deaf to anything you wish to say to me, or if there is anyone I am not listening to whom I should hear.
>
> Take my hands; if there is anything I could do that I am not doing, then set them about doing it.
>
> Take my tongue, to speak your words where you want them spoken. In a crisis, give me the words to say, as Jesus promised would happen.

---

15. John Milton (1608–1674), 'On his blindness'.

They also serve

Take my mind, to think your thoughts.

Take my heart, to love what you love and to stay humble.

Last of all, please take my feet. If I am in the wrong place, then take control of my feet and direct them to where you want me to be. Where I am may be right for today but less good for tomorrow, so in that case move me! I want to be where your Spirit can most happily breathe through me.

Please signal clearly, Holy God, because unless you do, I can only presume that what I am already doing is what you want, and I will do it with all my heart.

NINETY-SEVEN

Mighty warrior

Judges 6:11-18

Imagine the surprise of Gideon when the angel of the Lord appeared to him and greeted him with those words, 'The Lord is with you, you mighty warrior.' At the time, Gideon was beating out the wheat crop in his wine press, so that his enemies the Midianites would not spot the dust of the chaff rising and come and steal his wheat. Far from being a mighty warrior at the time, he was lying low and trying to stay out of trouble.

Yet the angel knew what he was talking about, and the 'mighty warrior' description came true soon afterwards. God believes in us more than we dare to believe in ourselves, and we have to be patient to see the promises of God happen. Take the gospel story of Peter, the apostle chosen by Jesus and given the new name Cephas, meaning Rock. At times Peter was anything but rock-like. He was boastful, intent on being the leader; he was going to be faithful to Jesus even if all the others ran away. But of course he turned out to be one of the weakest, keen to stay with Jesus as far as the courtyard of the high priest but then unable to state bravely who he was and what he was doing there at the fire (Mark 14:66-72).

Peter became Rock at that fire, refined to see himself in all his weakness, but nonetheless forgiven by Jesus. If Jesus' love and affection for him could survive even a shameful betrayal, then he knew that same love and affection was guaranteed for all time, and he need no longer fear his own weakness. The dross was gone; pure gold was left.

We may wish God would send an angel to call each of us by a special name, something true that God would then make come true. There is an exercise that you might like to try: imagine you are designing a coat of arms just for yourself. Usually a coat of arms has various symbols on the shield, and underneath is a word or a few words that are the family motto. If you were designing one just for yourself, what would be the motto that you would choose?

There is no shortage of attractive mottoes: Be still and know; Do not be afraid; My heart ever faithful; Good shepherd; Handmaid of the Lord; Faithful messenger; To set the prisoners free; My heart is restless (until it finds rest in you); I come to do your will; Jesus yesterday, today, forever; Different drum; Your servant, ready for anything; and so on – there are as many as there are people. If this idea pleases you, you could choose one for yourself; but best to be flexible. If tomorrow you do not like the motto you chose for yourself today, then pick another one that makes more sense.

This exercise helps to give a self-image that is positive, and it offers an ideal to live for. And God has a way of making our hopes and dreams come true even through what looks like failure. Gideon became a mighty warrior by going to war and winning, but Peter became a Rock initially by failing. Above all, Jesus fulfilled all the names that were prophesied about him when it looked as though he had failed miserably.

NINETY-EIGHT

To the bottom of the sea

Micah 7:19

The prophet Micah says confidently to God, 'You will cast all our sins into the depths of the sea'. God in his compassion will remove our sins from the sight of the rest of the human race and dump them in the deepest depth of the ocean. This is the same Micah who in the previous chapter told us exactly and simply what God wishes of us, namely 'to do justice, and to love kindness, and to walk humbly with your God' (Micah 6:8). For Micah, God is a God of compassion who will get rid of our sins and then give us a simple, straightforward way to go.

For the people of Israel in Old Testament times, the sea was a place of dread. They were not a sea-going nation like the Phoenicians who lived beside the Mediterranean Sea and who roamed far and wide in ships. The Jews in those days preferred dry land. So to picture our sins being thrown into the deepest depths of this watery grave where nobody ever wanted to go was a great relief. Even today, more than 2000 years later, no human being has managed to reach the bottom of the deepest oceans. The likes of Jacques Cousteau in a bathyscope have been far down, but not yet to the deepest depth there is. There are rumours of strange blind beasts, but nobody is down there, able to bring our sins back to the surface. Micah is still right: our sins will be safely got rid of.

Even better, of course, would be if the sins of our past were to disappear altogether: 'though your sins are like scarlet, they shall be like snow; though they are red like crimson, they shall become like wool,' are the words Isaiah attributes to God (Isaiah 1:18). As long as our sins are lurking in the depths of the sea, they are not as safe as if they were to disappear altogether. It is possible to pray for a day when I start completely afresh with God, when my sins will be never called to mind. The mystical holy woman Julian of Norwich saw in her revelations that God was never angry in the first place, but that the Lord loved as if nothing had ever separated us from him.

More traditionally, though, the best way to think of ourselves is as 'forgiven sinners'. I am a sinner; I have sinned and probably will sin again, but God's forgiveness is permanent, and I can indeed start each day afresh with no less love from God than yesterday.

As forgiven sinners, we can face the world and try again every time. If people we may have hurt object to our new confidence, we can only refer them to God: 'God has forgiven me and made me welcome in his kingdom. You, like the elder brother of the prodigal son, have the option to forgive me as well.'

To go along with Micah, where we started, perhaps best of all is to believe that God has forgiven me completely, but to keep me humble I remember that my sins were real, and I am grateful that they are not just forgiven, but they are also far removed from other people's sight.

NINETY-NINE

Prepared for siege

2 Chronicles 32:30

When Hezekiah was king in Jerusalem he performed a very clever piece of engineering, the works of which are still in operation today. The city was under constant threat from the armies of the Assyrian empire, and the city would be vulnerable if there were to be a siege. There was no constant source of water within the walls. The best well was the spring Gihon, which was outside the city walls. What Hezekiah set in motion was a tunnel to run underground and under the walls, channelling the water from the spring into the Pool of Siloam within the citadel. Then he had the spring Gihon completely hidden so that an enemy would not know there was a spring there at all. The siege army would be without water, and the citadel of Jerusalem would have an endless supply (see also 2 Kings 20:20).

The engineering works went well: men with pickaxes worked their way through the rock from both ends, from the spring outside and from the pool inside the walls. The wall of the tunnel still shows the chiselled rejoicings where the two excavation parties met: 'Here we came pick to pick!' No mean feat.

When the Assyrian army came to lay siege to Jerusalem, the city walls were strong (Hezekiah had strengthened them in readiness). The foreign troops waited for the citizens of Jerusalem to starve, but instead it was the foreigners – the Assyrians – who cracked first, because they had no water supply. After some time they gave up the siege very suddenly, overnight: it seems likely they were suffering heavily from dysentery and had to withdraw to Assyria. The city of Jerusalem remained secure for another hundred years after that attempt on its life.

I find this story rich in imagery for the spiritual life of any person in any age. We can all picture ourselves as a city surrounded by walls. In troubled times it seems that the city is threatened, and we wonder if our defences will hold out. Then, like Hezekiah's Jerusalem, we need a faithful water supply. Food shortages we can cope with, but water is the spring of life, and that we cannot do without.

Where is the water to be found that will see us through the times of trouble? Jesus spoke about living water (running water) welling up from the ground and offered it to the woman at the well (John 4:10). What exactly did Jesus mean?

I would say he meant forgiveness. Once I know myself lovingly forgiven by God, I can stand anything else that life throws at me. Like water, it may not seem much, but God's forgiveness is life giving, making it worthwhile to get out of bed each morning and carry on the fight. When I have forgiveness and the forces of sadness outside my city do not believe in forgiveness, their days are numbered.

ONE HUNDRED

Love in return for love

John 15:9

In the end, there are only two things to ask God for: first, to know myself to be loved and forgiven by God, and secondly to have the strength to love God back. If I have those, then I need nothing more.

We have a tendency to forget how many loving gifts we have from God. It is a worthwhile exercise to recall them, and to recall the love of the giver. God gives me the sun, the moon and the stars, and a place under the sun. He gives me life, breath and the air we breathe; he gives gravity to keep me from falling off the world as it spins. His gifts include the plants, the animals and the birds in all their amazing variety. He gives me my body, and in my case the ability to walk, run and swim; my hands, without which life would be so difficult; my eyes, which have been faithful servants for so many years, and my ears and my tongue. I have had parents to bring me up so patiently, and friends and neighbours. Not everybody has all of these, but we all have many of them, and they are gifts. I did not have to do anything to qualify as a human being and to live on the planet Earth.

As a baptised Christian, I have been given a relationship with God as my Father, something over and above just having God as my creator. The Bible is a priceless gift, as is the membership of a church, where everybody treats everyone else as a brother or a sister. I have Jesus the Son of God as my brother, risen and present with me in so many ways. I have forgiveness from God, through Jesus and the cross he carried for me. I have the gift of prayer, of being able to believe in God's goodness and of being able to talk to God in an intimate way.

When it comes to my personal gifts – things given to me and not to others – the list grows even longer. As human beings we all share many gifts, but each of us has unique gifts. Other people have eyes, but no one else besides me looks out at the world through my two eyes or the rest of my senses. There are some things I am good at doing that many other people cannot do, and they have their own gifts. Some people are funny, some people can dance; some people can make music with instruments, some people can sing, some people have skills with athletics and sport, some people are good at crosswords or at mathematics.

I know not everybody has all of these things, but if we count our blessings rather than counting what we don't have, the list is still impressive. Over and above all that, we have God dwelling in us as in a temple, and this is a gift that outweighs all the other gifts. Holy God has been preparing this Earth for me over countless light years, and for millions of years developing the planet to where it can sustain you and me. Every little thing in this world speaks of the love of God, if we only had eyes to see.

I pray that we may see the love of God behind all these gifts, and I pray for the strength of the Holy Spirit to enable us to love God in return, through a life of faithful service.

Index of Scripture references

Reference	Page	Title
Genesis 3:24	92	A sword to guard the way
Leviticus 15:19-30	14	Clean
Judges 6:11-18	97	Mighty warrior
Ruth 1:16, 17	81	'Where you go, I will go'
1 Kings 17:7-16	55	One day at a time
1 Kings 18:20-40	77	Water and fire
2 Chronicles 32:30	99	Prepared for siege
Psalm 123	96	They also serve
Isaiah 1:18	58	From scarlet to white as snow
Isaiah 40:28-31	88	Wings like eagles
Jonah 4:11	74	Left hand, right hand
Micah 7:19	98	To the bottom of the sea
Matthew 2:1-12	25	The star comes and goes
Matthew 3:13-15	11	Jesus' baptism and mine
Matthew 5:14-16	30	Shine a light
Matthew 5:21, 22	79	Calling people names
Matthew 6:26	84	Your Father feeds them
Matthew 7:13, 14	27	The narrow gate
Matthew 7:24-7	33	The house built on rock
Matthew 10:8	65	Give without payment
Matthew 10:11-14	61	Peace comes back
Matthew 10:30	95	The hairs of your head
Matthew 11:25-30	9	'Come to me . . .'
Matthew 13:24-30	18	Weeds among the wheat
Matthew 13:44	91	Treasure hidden in a field
Matthew 14:28-33	51	Peter fears the waves
Matthew 17:1-8	12	Transfiguration
Matthew 17:24-7	63	No taxes for the children
Matthew 18:3	28	Change and become like children
Matthew 18:21, 22	21	How many times?
Matthew 18:23-35	65	Give without payment
Matthew 20:1-16	45	'I am generous'
Matthew 22:1-14	94	Wedding robe
Matthew 25:1-13	41	Ten bridesmaids
Matthew 25:14-30	1	Talents: a point of view
Matthew 25:40	64	If they all went away . . .
Mark 1:9-11	11	Jesus' baptism and mine
Mark 1:10, 12, 18, 20, 21, 23, 28-30, 42, 43	70	'Immediately'

Mark 2:1-12	3	Raising the roof
Mark 2:21, 22	37	Old and new
Mark 3:13-19	2	Jesus chooses his apostles
Mark 3:35	72	Brother, sister and mother
Mark 4:1-20	8	Birds, rock, thorns, good soil
Mark 4:35-41	73	Two kinds of desolation
Mark 5:1-20	4	Legion of demons
Mark 5:24-34	14	Clean
Mark 6:14-29	38	John beheaded
Mark 6:30-52	15	The promised Shepherd
Mark 6:48	54	Walking on water
Mark 7:27	75	Own place at the table
Mark 8:1-10	6	Feeding the four thousand
Mark 9:14-29	36	The boy cured of epilepsy
Mark 11:12-14	56	Tree always in fruit
Mark 12:28-34	82	Not far
Mark 13:2	76	Stone upon stone
Mark 14:35	13	'*Abba!*'
	16	If it were possible
Mark 15:37-8	52	Temple curtain torn
Mark 16:1, 2	57	Holy Week and Easter
Luke 1:35	78	The Holy Spirit will come
Luke 1:46-55	20	Nothingness blessed
Luke 3:23	17	Jesus: the hidden years
Luke 6:37	23	'Do not judge . . .'
	48	You will be forgiven
Luke 9:57, 58	22	No fixed abode
Luke 10:29-37	40	Jesus good Samaritan
Luke 10:38-42	10	Martha and Mary
Luke 11:2	13	'*Abba!*'
Luke 12:8, 9	7	The last word?
Luke 13:10-17	5	Bent double
Luke 14:7-11	86	Places at table
Luke 14:12-14	83	When you give a banquet
Luke 15:11-32	19	Even better than being good
Luke 17:11-19	53	Grateful leper
Luke 18:9-14	34	Who is right?
Luke 22:19, 20	31	Bread, then wine
John 1:42	35	Peter the Rock
John 2:1-11	26	Wine and water
John 8:32	32	'The truth will make you free'
John 14:2	39	Many inns
John 14:27	59	Two kinds of peace
John 15:9	100	Love in return for love
John 15:12	89	Gift and invitation

Index of Scripture references

John 16:12-15	87	When the Spirit of truth comes
John 20:16	43	Recognising Jesus risen
John 20:21-3	90	To forgive or to retain?
John 21:15	29	'Feed my lambs'
Acts 3:14, 15	50	About Bar'abbas
Acts 4:27-30	49	'. . . your holy servant Jesus'
Romans 8:28	66	All is well?
1 Corinthians 13:4-9	46	God is . . . love is
1 Corinthians 15:3-8	44	Christ died for our sins
2 Corinthians 8:9	42	Jesus became poor
Galatians 2:6	67	God shows no partiality
Ephesians 1:4, 5	93	Before the foundation
Ephesians 3:20, 21	47	More than
Ephesians 4:31–5:2	85	Be imitators of God
2 Timothy 4:14, 15	24	Alexander the coppersmith
Hebrews 10:18	69	All sins forgiven
Hebrews 12:1	71	Cloud of witnesses
Hebrews 12:23	68	Firstborn
1 Peter 1:7, 18, 19	80	Precious
1 John 4:8	62	God is love
Revelation 21:15, 16	60	Only a few saved?

Thematic index

Jesus' death and resurrection
43 Recognising Jesus risen
44 Christ died for our sins
49 '. . . your holy servant Jesus'
50 About Bar'abbas
52 Temple curtain torn
56 Tree always in fruit
57 Holy Week and Easter
92 A sword to guard the way

The life of Jesus
17 Jesus: the hidden years
70 'Immediately'
81 'Where you go, I will go'

Teaching and ministry of Jesus
1   Talents: a point of view
8   Birds, rock, thorns, good soil
9   'Come to me . . .'
18 Weeds among the wheat
19 Even better than being good
27 The narrow gate
28 Change and become like children
30 Shine a light
32 'The truth will make you free'
33 The house built on rock
34 Who is right?
37 Old and new
39 Many inns
40 Jesus good Samaritan
41 Ten bridesmaids
56 Tree always in fruit
59 Two kinds of peace
63 No taxes for the children
64 If they all went away . . .
76 Stone upon stone
79 Calling people names
80 Precious
82 Not far
83 When you give a banquet
86 Places at table
87 When the Spirit of truth comes
91 Treasure hidden in a field
94 Wedding robe
95 The hairs of your head
100 Love in return for love

Miracles
3   Raising the roof
4   Legion of demons
5   Bent double
6   Feeding the four thousand
14 Clean
15 The promised Shepherd
26 Wine and water
36 The boy cured of epilepsy
50 About Bar'abbas
51 Peter fears the waves
53 Grateful leper
54 Walking on water
55 One day at a time
73 Two kinds of desolation
77 Water and fire

Poverty and riches
8   Birds, rock, thorns, good soil
22 No fixed abode
42 Jesus became poor

Shepherds and sheep
15 The promised Shepherd
29 'Feed my lambs'
89 Gift and invitation

God's grace and forgiveness
3   Raising the roof
7   The last word?
19 Even better than being good
21 How many times?
23 'Do not judge . . .'

Thematic index

24 Alexander the coppersmith
27 The narrow gate
29 'Feed my lambs'
33 The house built on rock
34 Who is right?
35 Peter the Rock
37 Old and new
44 Christ died for our sins
45 'I am generous'
47 More than
48 You will be forgiven
58 From scarlet to white as snow
65 Give without payment
69 All sins forgiven
74 Left hand, right hand
79 Calling people names
88 Wings like eagles
90 To forgive or to retain?
92 A sword to guard the way
98 To the bottom of the sea
99 Prepared for siege

The family of God/God as Father
11 Jesus' baptism and mine
13 'Abba!'
28 Change and become like children
32 'The truth will make you free'
33 The house built on rock
41 Ten bridesmaids
52 Temple curtain torn
60 Only a few saved?
63 No taxes for the children
67 God shows no partiality
68 Firstborn
71 Cloud of witnesses
72 Brother, sister and mother
75 Own place at the table
78 The Holy Spirit will come
80 Precious
83 When you give a banquet
84 Your Father feeds them
85 Be imitators of God
87 When the Spirit of truth comes
93 Before the foundation
95 The hairs of your head

Judgement
7   The last word?
18 Weeds among the wheat
23 'Do not judge . . .'
48 You will be forgiven
79 Calling people names
90 To forgive or to retain?

Eternity
22 No fixed abode
39 Many inns
60 Only a few saved?
68 Firstborn
86 Places at table
93 Before the foundation

Love
16 If it were possible
27 The narrow gate
33 The house built on rock
46 God is . . . love is
54 Walking on water
62 God is love
67 God shows no partiality
71 Cloud of witnesses
82 Not far
85 Be imitators of God
88 Wings like eagles
89 Gift and invitation
100 Love in return for love

Compassion
5   Bent double
6   Feeding the four thousand
40 esus good Samaritan
74 Left hand, right hand

Comfort and consolation
4   Legion of demons
5   Bent double
9   'Come to me . . .'
25 The star comes and goes
43 Recognising Jesus risen
54 Walking on water
59 Two kinds of peace

215

64 If they all went away . . .
66 All is well?
73 Two kinds of desolation
75 Own place at the table
84 Your Father feeds them

Healing and acceptance
14 Clean
40 Jesus good Samaritan
53 Grateful leper
58 From scarlet to white as snow

Gifts of God
19 Even better than being good
20 Nothingness blessed
26 Wine and water
53 Grateful leper
84 Your Father feeds them
86 Places at table
91 Treasure hidden in a field
94 Wedding robe
100 Love in return for love

Generosity
20 Nothingness blessed
22 No fixed abode
38 John beheaded
42 Jesus became poor
45 'I am generous'
47 More than
68 Firstborn
83 When you give a banquet

Baptism
4   Legion of demons
11 Jesus' baptism and mine
12 Transfiguration
30 Shine a light
32 'The truth will make you free'
75 Own place at the table
77 Water and fire

Eucharist/communion
6   Feeding the four thousand
26 Wine and water
31 Bread, then wine

The Holy Spirit
41 Ten bridesmaids
70 'Immediately'
77 Water and fire
78 The Holy Spirit will come
87 When the Spirit of truth comes
90 To forgive or to retain?

Prayer and contemplation
10 Martha and Mary
13 '*Abba!*'
36 The boy cured of epilepsy
51 Peter fears the waves

Christian life and mission
2   Jesus chooses his apostles
27 The narrow gate
29 'Feed my lambs'
32 'The truth will make you free'
49 '. . . your holy servant Jesus'
55 One day at a time
61 Peace comes back
65 Give without payment
72 Brother, sister and mother
76 Stone upon stone
81 'Where you go, I will go'
89 Gift and invitation
96 They also serve
97 Mighty warrior
99 Prepared for siege

Community/relationships
2   Jesus chooses his apostles
24 Alexander the coppersmith